Minds in Motion

Minds in Motion

The Nonverbals of Subliminal Influence

RENÉ-MARC MANGIN

Library of Congress Control Number:		2005907595
ISBN 10:	Hardcover	1-59926-515-X
	Softcover	1-59926-514-1
ISBN 13:	Hardcover	978-1-59926-515-5
	Softcover	978-1-59926-514-8

This book was printed in the United States of America.

To order additional copies of this book, contact:
Xlibris Corporation
1-888-795-4274
www.Xlibris.com
Orders@Xlibris.com
28925

Contents

Introduction

Nonverbal communication is no longer synonymous with "body language." The term "body language" became part of popular culture a quarter of a century ago when Julius Fast wrote a bestseller entitled "Body Language." The body language described in Fast's book was based on research on courting rituals. Knowledge about nonverbal behavior has progressed a great deal along two tracks since the 1970s. The most recognized track is reading nonverbal behavior – something that agencies like the U.S. Custom Service and the FBI have refined significantly. FBI special agent, Joe Navarro, a lecturer on nonverbal behavior explains its status with the following statement, "We believe the study of nonverbal behavior has progressed to such a degree that in capable hands, it is now more accurate than lie-detector tests" (Davis, Pereira and Bulkeley, 2002). The second track involves the use of nonverbal behavior to affect others. We will explore how this is accomplished subliminally using "fixed action patterns."

Skill in reading and influencing people is the difference between being good and being best in many professions. This may seem obvious in poker playing, sales, and political campaigning but nonverbal skills are also critical for trial lawyers, physicians and mediators. The following are firsthand accounts of how nonverbal behavior affects each of these professions.

The importance of nonverbal behavior in mediation became evident to me after transcribing the audiotapes of a negotiation I had successfully mediated between county commissioners from neighboring counties as a graduate school project in discourse analysis. I was expecting to be able to identify language that informed the mediator (me) that the parties had softened their positions or were interested in finding common ground. I knew that I had responded to something, and I thought it was language. Much to my surprise, after producing highly detailed transcripts (noting all the pauses, ums, overlapping speech, etc.), I could find nothing in the language of the negotiators. Years later, it became apparent that skilled mediators seem to unconsciously respond to changes in gaze behavior, muscle tone, and voice patterns, as well as shifts in the body positions of negotiators.

Lately, physicians have been focusing a great deal of attention on doctor-patient communication as a means of improving healthcare delivery and reducing the likelihood of being sued. In 2002, physicians at an annual conference sponsored by The Center for Medical Excellence in Portland, Oregon were surprised to hear Dr. Wendy Levinson, chairwoman of the School of Medicine at the University of Toronto, report that research she and colleagues had conducted at Harvard (2002) indicated a strong correlation between a physician's tone of voice and being sued. After masking the words being spoken by surgeons, researchers found that tone of voice was a strong indicator of which of them would be sued. Unfortunately, Dr. Levinson then suggested that little that could be done to change someone's tone—which is wrong. Tone and inflection are critical aspects of nonverbal behavior and people can be trained to modify them relatively easily.

A question by Dr. Barry Dorn, an orthopedic surgeon and professor at Tufts Medical School and in the Harvard Healthcare Negotiation Program, highlighted the importance of nonverbal behavior regarding bedside manner. Dr. Dorn approached me after a presentation I had given on nonverbal behavior in Toronto. He asked me if nonverbal behavior could be the reason why several of his patients had raved about one of his interns. They reported that the intern was very caring, attentive, and spent a great deal of time with them. Being curious about the patients' responses, Dr. Dorn sought to figure out what the young physician was doing. He found that the intern did not spend any more time with patients than other physicians, and that he did not seem to do anything particularly unique. Dr. Dorn was perplexed. As we discussed the intern's behavior, Barry recalled the intern's relaxed demeanor and that he made more physical contact (often indirect) with the patients than other physicians. It turned out that the intern's nonverbal behavior (breathing, touch, and eye contact) calmed patients and distorted their perception of time.

The intern was not spending more time with patients, but in fact was spending "quality time" with them. He was connecting with them kinesthetically, thereby subliminally sowing the seeds for warm doctor-patient relationships. These favorable relationships not only improved the prospects for a good prognosis, but also diminished the likelihood of his being sued if things turned out badly since people tend not to sue friends. A review of 25 surveys on doctor-patient interactions in the March 10, 2001 issue of The Lancet reported that good bedside manners and warm doctor-patient relationships contributed favorably to the outcome of medical care (Adams, 2005).

The importance of nonverbal behavior in a courtroom is obvious to any astute observer of the remarkably successful trial lawyer, Gerry Spence. A one-day Continuing Legal Education course with Gerry Spence at the University of Washington School of Law in the mid-1990s, led me to conclude that Mr. Spence is a master of subliminal influence. His ability to read the nonverbal behaviors of jurors (unconsciously) and address their concerns in real-time is truly remarkable.

Mr. Spence's lecture stressed the importance of connecting with jurors. He explained that the jury does not care about a lawyer's legal pedigree, evidentiary procedure, or other legal nuances. He asserted that understanding the jury, and presenting your case in a way that makes sense to it, by using your inherent abilities to connect with it determine success in the courtroom. The high points of his presentation occurred during his impromptu demonstrations of opening arguments, efforts to frame his case during voir dire, and summations. The substance of what he was saying and his nonverbal behavior seemed to be elegantly choreographed for maximum effect. He used phrasing and his voice to paint "word pictures" infused with emotion. His posture, gestures, and movements, as well as timing, were all designed for effect.

On a strategic level, Gerry Spence's nonverbal behaviors were perfectly matched with his image, physical characteristics, and objectives. He structured his appeals to juries around their deep values, delivered them in a baritone voice with almost choreographed movements and gestures, and punctuated by strategic pauses.

Gerry Spence establishes a relationship with jurors, and they consequently feel what he says to them. He understands that commitment to a verdict is not as much about logic as it is about feelings.

Spence has given a lot of thought to his courtroom performance but even he does not seem to have a systematic knowledge of his nonverbal behavior. He intuits what to do much like the young physician and or a skilled mediator. I liken working intuitively to being like a natural hitter in baseball. A natural hitter is great when he is "hot," but can rarely pull himself out of a slump because he doesn't know what to correct. He never had to figure out how to hit the ball, so when he stops hitting the ball he doesn't know where to start to fix things. Someone who has studied the mechanics of hitting, on the other hand, can systematically make adjustments to improve his performance.

This book is designed to help systematize a professional's performance by providing practical information about four basic patterns of thinking and communication, the implications of those patterns, and defining some key principles about nonverbal behavior that make it possible to subliminally influence people successfully and consistently.

Minds in Motion presents new insights about reading people and nonverbally asserting subliminal influence. The material in this book is based on new research on the mind-body connection and its impact on nonverbal behavior and communication. Two major changes in scientific thinking have advanced knowledge in nonverbal communication and behavior. The first significant change is based on the work of physician researcher, Antonio Damasio (1994), who has proved the inseparable link between feelings and thinking. In his book *Descartes Error*, he explains that René Descartes' statement, "I think therefore I am" should be restated to read, "I feel therefore I am." And he makes the point that anything you feel is registered in your body. In a later work, Damasio explains that humans use emotions to react effectively to critical situations and to think. He also asserts that the biological expression of emotions is universal (sadness is expressed the same way for a Swede, a Peruvian, and an Australian aborigine); that emotional responses are automatic and involuntary (they happen beyond our control); and that emotions are observable because they "use the body as a theater" (Damasio, 1999:51). The second important and complementary change occurred when the concept of nonverbal communication was expanded to include people's involuntary actions and behaviors, as well as, the voluntary actions of "body language" such as gestures and postures.

Using involuntary nonverbal behavior as a form of communication is not a new idea. Paul Ekman (1992) has studied deception by observing the actions of involuntary muscles in people's faces for years. In fact, the University of California at San Francisco psychologist published a standardized system for analyzing facial expressions called the Facial Action Coding System (FACS) in 1978. Dr. Ekman's work is based on the fact that the brains of all people are similarly wired to the muscles under the skin of the face. "Our lips get thinner when we're angry. Our blink rate increases when we're nervous. Our eyes widen with excitement or fear. Our nostrils flare when we're aroused, and blood flow increases, reddening our skin when we're preparing for a fight, whether it's of a physical or mental nature. It is hard to suppress these expressions, Dr. Ekman maintains, because they emanate from areas of the brain that control many of the involuntary muscles" (Davis, Pereira and Bulkeley, 2002:4). Many elite law enforcement agencies use this system and his methods for detecting deception. While reading facial gestures may not be new, attaching meaning to involuntary actions in the rest of the body is. It is only recently that researchers have acknowledged that brains are also wired to involuntary muscles and organs throughout the body, and therefore can be used to read brain activity.

Nonverbal behaviors provide a skilled observer with much more information than what is needed to identify smugglers, terrorists, and liars. Recent research indicates that watching someone's nonverbal behavior can determine how he thinks (linear or by association, or with pictures, words, or feelings), and how he feels about an idea in real-time – without him ever saying anything. She also can discern how he processes and stores information, as well as, some of his key values based on his nonverbal behaviors. In summary, the information derived from current law enforcement strategies for reading nonverbal behavior is rudimentary and narrow compared to what is available.

The use of nonverbal behavior to influence others is also covered in *Minds in Motion*. Subliminal influence can be applied in two situations. In one the audience is a passive receiver, and in the other there is interplay between a "speaker-sender" and a "listener-perceiver." Members of television audiences and audiences at rallies or lectures are passive receivers because there is little "give and take" between a speaker or sender of messages and them. The terms "speaker-sender" and "listener-perceiver" are used to acknowledge that senders of messages often send both verbal and nonverbal signals, and listeners often perceive signals with more just than their eyes. The reality of interpersonal interactions is that we are always sending and receiving nonverbal messages, even if we are consciously unaware of either activity. We are typically unaware of the signals we are sending, and even though we respond to nonverbal signals, we are rarely consciously aware of having received them.

The current use of nonverbals to detect deception and suspicious people, or to create impressions are one-way applications of nonverbals. In these cases, someone is sending a message to modify behavior, or receiving messages that someone else is trying to hide. The use of nonverbal influence currently emphasizes the design and delivery of a message to influence a passive audience. These one-way transactions are used to change behavior, thinking, or decision making in a target audience. Target audiences are typically television viewers of TV advertisements, juries in opening or closing arguments in court, people at rallies, or television news viewers. Advertisers, marketers and mass media specialists have taken advantage of advances in technology and applied research in behavioral psychology and perception to capture "eyeballs" and greatly increase the persuasive power of commercials, propaganda, and political advertisements. Depending on the medium, they use visual, auditory or kinesthetic stimuli to influence members of their audiences.

Consultants and marketers seek to understand the perceptual and cognitive processes of a target audience because they know that such knowledge greatly enhances the prospects for using nonverbal influence to manipulate its understanding of reality. Attempts to influence consumers and voters nonverbally are now ubiquitous. They can take the form of subtle swooshing sounds to create a sense of dynamism as data is presented on a TV screen during a football game, jerky handheld camera shots to create the impression of movement or chaos, printed words on backdrops positioned strategically behind politicians at press conferences to reinforce their message, or the choreographed repetition of pithy stock phrases like "war on terror" designed to trigger emotional responses that override logic in specific audiences.

Some of the most elegant applications of one-way nonverbal influence are being executed in politics. Michael Deaver, former Reagan (and now Bush) communications advisor, used his knowledge of nonverbals to manipulate TV news coverage of his candidate and his policies. He did so by furnishing networks with visually appealing footage for their stories. Even seasoned journalists like Leslie Stahl did not understand how they were being used. In her case, she confessed her confusion about why the Reagan administration continued to send her prime footage for her reports when many of her stories highlighted the negative impacts of his policies. Deaver explained that as long as she was using the footage that he provided, he didn't care what she said because his message was drowning out hers (Moyers, 1989).

Deaver understood the power of visual memory over auditory memory. The following exchange between Deaver and Bill Moyers reveals Michael Deaver's perspective on the use nonverbal cues.

Moyers: In the competition between the eye and the ear, your judgment is . . . ?

Deaver: The eye wins every time.

The power of television has made image management the most important aspect of political campaigning. In 1989, journalist and media critic Bill Moyers, concluded that, "Visual images are the new language of politics." Understanding which nonverbals have the most potency and create lasting effects is critical to strategically and effectively using nonverbals for subliminal influence.

Political consultants work very hard to create powerful images and impressions because they know that when it comes time to vote, people generally remember visual images and associated feelings, not government actions and policy statements. To elaborate, they remember the impressions they have of a person long after they have forgotten the actions that created those impressions. This may be why a Republican advisor insisted that former FEMA director, Mike "Brownie" Brown, roll up his sleeves at press conferences during the hurricane Katrina debacle. Looking like he was working hard in front of the cameras was supposed to counter the reality of substantively doing very little.

Much of the material in *Minds in Motion* pertains to subliminal influence in two-way communications. Two-way transactions are more complicated than one-way interactions, but are also characteristic of the majority of people's everyday interactions. Two-way transactions are complicated by pairings of actions and responses as people both send and receive messages in social interactions. "Speaker-senders" become "listener-perceivers" and vice versa during these interactions. They are also of interest to professionals service providers, such as lawyers interacting with clients, physicians interacting with customers.

The essence of influence in a two-way communication is the ability to manage one's own nonverbal behavior to affect the behaviors of others. In the past ten years, clients concerned with influence in two-way transactions have included: teachers, government regulators, physicians, mediators, and salespeople. The art of nonverbal influence in two-way communications requires understanding how our behaviors affect others and reading the nonverbal responses of listener-perceivers.

Nonverbal influence in two-way transactions also requires the ability to perceive what others are doing as others modify behaviors in response to yours. It is important to be able to observe and be able to respond to changes in heart rate, the rate and nature of respiration, muscle tone and skin color changes, and unconscious small-scale movements that are almost instantaneous and generally beyond the control of speakers and listeners. Observing these responses does not require high tech instruments; instead it requires the sensory acuity developed through training and practice.

Minds in Motion introduces a new concept called a "fixed action pattern" into the realm of nonverbal commuication. A fixed action pattern (a FAP) is an automatic, reflex behavior in response to a nonverbal cue. It is particularly powerful because it influences a listener-perceiver's behavior without his or her conscious awareness. Subliminal influence depends on FAPs.

New insights about perception, cognitive processing, and nonverbal behavior have made it possible to understand and appreciate dynamic, two-way interactions. The effect of these insights has been to make it possible for a skilled speaker-sender to manage his or her nonverbals to influence a listener-perceiver subliminally, interactively, and in real-time.

The Researcher's View of Nonverbal Communication

Nonverbal communication accomplishes three things that make it powerful from a communications perspective. First, it can *purposefully* convey meaning. In others words, it can be used effectively to inform, instruct, entertain, or persuade. Second, it can *accurately* convey meaning, although accuracy varies according to the type of nonverbal behavior. For example, a facial gesture is probably more accurate at conveying meaning than touch. Finally, it *efficiently* communicates meaning. Tears welling up in your eyes during a sad movie communicate that you are experiencing an intense emotion more efficiently than almost any words.

Communications professionals have only recently started to focus a great deal of attention on nonverbal communications. In fact, the National Communication Association only recently decided to create a section devoted to it. Leathers (1992:3, 4) explains that nonverbal communication has great functional significance for six major reasons:

1. Nonverbal, not verbal factors are the major determinants of meaning in an interpersonal context.
2. Feelings and emotions are more accurately revealed by nonverbal than verbal means.
3. The nonverbal portion of communication conveys meanings and intentions that are relatively free of deception and distortion.
4. Nonverbal cues can serve to clarify the intent and meaning of a message and take precedence in the mind of the receiver of the message.
5. Nonverbal cues represent a much more efficient (communicate more in less time) means of communicating than verbal cues.
6. Nonverbal cues represent the most suitable vehicle for suggestion.

The final three points are related to the persuasive power of nonverbal behavior. Ethnographic research indicates that nonverbal cues can actually override a concurrent verbal message. Most of us have heard someone say something like, "I am confident that I will be acquitted" and noted that we were not convinced. It is likely that the nonverbal part of the person's message (for example, tone, posture, facial expression) contradicted his or her words.

A skilled speaker-sender can intentionally send a nonverbal message that is different than what he is saying. Unskilled speaker-senders often unintentionally send nonverbal signals that contradict their verbal messages. For example, teachers will commonly tell students that everyone must sit down while standing up. His or her nonverbal behavior is subliminally telling the student that not everyone has to sit.

Nonverbal communication can be much more efficient than verbal communication. It is often necessary to repeat important ideas, but pictures tend to stick in people's minds. Additionally, a picture presents a great deal of information very quickly and often provides less opportunity for interpretation errors than speech. Pictures are also easier to remember than words. These two features of pictures may explain why most major trial consulting firms have large graphics departments.

Subliminal messages are suggestions, and like hypnotic suggestions, they rely greatly on nonverbal channels for transmission and reception. "The nature of a communication situation often dictates that ideas and emotions can be more effectively expressed indirectly than directly" (Leathers, 1992:9). Many nonverbal messages communicate below the normal level of awareness. "They act on the subconscious mind, exerting a powerful influence on how we think, feel and behave without our ever being aware of exactly what is producing those reactions" (Lewis, 1989:9).

This book is organized in three sections: background information about nonverbal behavior and related sciences; the art of reading nonverbals and what they mean; and how to use nonverbals to influence others. The first section explains why physiological responses are so important to new notions of nonverbal behavior. The second section presents a strategy for reading nonverbal behavior to learn how people think and communicate, as well as, ascertaining value preferences. The information provided herein will enable a reader to increase the range and depth of the information obtained from social interactions. The third section presents seven key principles for using nonverbal behavior to influence others subliminally.

Mac versus DOS: Dueling Processors

The human brain is divided into specialized halves whose capabilities are well-documented (Springer and Deutsch, 1993; Howard, 1994). Each of these hemispheres has its own orientation and experiences reality differently. Notions of reality are usually produced by the interaction of these hemispheres, although one hemisphere is often dominant and therefore has more influence on your interpretation than the other. During a conversation, the left hemisphere generally responds to the literal meaning of the words it hears without much notice of inflection or tone. While the left hemisphere is paying attention to the words, the right hemisphere perceives tone of voice, facial expression, and body language of the person.

The hemispheres of the brain operate differently. In some important ways, the right hemisphere functions like a MacIntosh (Mac) computer and the left hemisphere like early IBM PCs that used a DOS. This comparison is simplistic, but meaningful. DOS is a software tool originally designed to create disk files, copy files, delete them, and organize them. This was accomplished by typing text commands on a black screen (White, 1999). The operating system of a computer serves like a mid-level manager. It posts the office rules that applications like Word and Excel must obey. These applications can be thought of as the office's top executives; they have bright ideas but don't have a clue about how to carry them out. The applications give vague instructions to the operating systems and the OS passes more detailed instructions to the "clerks" contained in another part of the computer called the BIOS.

In the mid-1980s Apple introduced the revolutionary MacIntosh computer to compete with established IBM and clone PCs. At that time the great majority of PCs were run by Microsoft DOS operating systems.

The Mac provided computer users with a means of managing disk files without being forced to type lines of text on a blank screen. It made it possible for people to operate a computer without using DOS. All you had to do was click onto one of many tiny cartoons to accomplish the same thing that required several lines of text commands in DOS.

The Mac quickly became the preferred tool of graphic artists, the DOS-driven PC was commonly associated with secretaries, engineers and scientists. In fact, it was the intuitive nature of the Mac that ultimately made the PC desirable to a mass audience (and forced Microsoft to create a similar operating system called Windows). People with little computer training could understand how to use a Mac in minutes. Today most PCs use the cartoon-driven (icon) system of the Mac or Microsoft Windows.

Even though there is no longer competition between Mac and DOS users in the PC world, Mac and DOS minds are still clashing. The Mac mind uses sensory images to think and operates intuitively. "Intuitive judgments are not arrived at step by step, but in an instant. It typically takes into consideration a large mass of data in parallel without separately considering each factor" (Blakeslee, 1980:25). It tends to be nonverbal and people operating in this mode prefer to communicate ideas via metaphors and analogies. The DOS mind operates in the opposite way. It is verbal (uses text), linear, and sequential. Commands have to be generated from the mind of the user as lines of consecutive text, whereas Mac commands are pre-positioned as an array of icons from which the user selects. Mac icons are pre-packaged routines requiring yes or no responses. Using them is fast and does not entail much deliberation. Problem solving for the DOS mind, on the other hand, involves focused, deliberate, sequential steps. It frames situations according to discrete rules and then a sequential, language-driven process to produce an answer. Relevant rules determine what can appear on the blank screen.

Humans seem predisposed to be right or left hemisphere dominant, and with that dominance comes aptitudes, interests. Dominance simply develops. People who rely on the right hemisphere of their brains to think and communicate tend to have "Mac brains." Their thinking and speech is nonverbal and nonlinear. In contrast, those who rely more heavily on the left hemisphere of their brains to perform these functions have DOS brains. They tend to think with words and appreciate linear, sequential thought and talk. It is not a matter of choice.

Each side of the brain does things in its own way. Processes within the hemispheres seem to take place in semi-isolated units that a research psychologist at MIT (Jerry Fodor) calls modules. These modules seem to be specialized for dealing with certain kinds of information and problems (Ehrlich, 2000:117). While the hemispheres have been studied regarding learning and classroom performance, the implications for interpersonal communications are still relatively unexplored.

Hemispheric specialization is very important in the process of reading nonverbals, and, exercising influence on others. Specific skills associated with each hemisphere are used at different times in reading or influencing others. Too much dependence on one hemisphere or the other can be an impediment to effectively performing either function. For example, relying on right hemisphere skills can make it easy to perceive what is going on in an interaction but make it difficult to understand it in a context beyond the immediate situation; thus making it difficult to act strategically. Effective strategic behavior often requires the analysis of data through time, but the right brain's focus on "being in the moment" and the use of "gut feelings" makes this type of analysis unlikely. Conversely, exclusive dependence on left hemisphere skills tends to enable brilliant analysis based on unnecessarily limited information and devoid of nonverbal cues. Furthermore, left-brained analysis requires that the person mentally remove himself or herself from the engagement, thus blinding them to what is going on.

Reading people requires the wide-open reception of the right brain, the analytical skills of the left brain to make correlations, and ultimately, the right brain's ability to identify patterns in behaviors. Influencing others often starts with left brain activities including the identification of a target audience, a setting in which to exercise influence, and an objective. Planning then is conducted by the left brain, but execution is best accomplished by the right brain. The right brain scans the environment and reacts in a coordinated fashion in real-time.

A brief exploration of how the right and left brain receives and express information follows. The right hemisphere receives information very differently than the left hemisphere. It processes a great deal more information than the left hemisphere, and it does so simultaneously. Strangely, much of its processing is unconscious. Even though the processing is largely unconscious, we are consciously aware of the impressions generated, and usually in a flash.

Reception versus Inputting

People who primarily receive information via the right hemisphere of the brain are fully aware of what is going on in the environment around them and pay attention to it. The right hemisphere deals with large elements of perception, general outlines of figures in the visual field, gross movements of limbs, and strong emotions. The left, by contrast, "generally specializes in fine analysis and precise movements (such as are involved in vocalization) and meanings" (Ehrlich, 2000:115). The right hemisphere seems to "receive" information, whereas the left hemisphere seems to "input" information.

When listening, right hemisphere dominant people are focusing their attention outwardly, but often not in an organized or systematic way. They take in visual, auditory, and kinesthetic aspects of what surrounds them leading some people to call them "externally-focused." The right hemisphere recognizes strong emotional cues and perceives in three dimensions, particularly noting the descriptive features of the other person's actions (talk and responses) including posture, eye contact, and gestures. It processes as a gestalt these variables instead of introspectively using existing assumptions to create meaning (Bodenhammer and Hall, 1997).

The right hemisphere dominant person is "handicapped in the world of words" (Freed and Parsons, 1997:53). The right hemisphere's inattention to the nuance of words and word order creates problems in comprehension and expression. Verbal meaning is largely determined by the *order* in which words occur. For example, "'Tom hits Bill' has a different meaning from 'Bill hits Tom.' In order to preserve meaning, our verbal memory must then preserve the order of sequences of words" (Blakeslee, 1980:38).

It is also not unusual for right-brained people to experience "auditory lag." For example, someone giving them instructions to execute a three step procedure might find that they understands all or part of the first step, almost entirely fail to register the second, and remember the last part of the third step. A person with auditory lag hears and understands most of step one, but is caught continuing to process step one as step two is being given. By the time he is ready to hear step 3 most of it has already been given. Step two is muddled by the last part of step one and the first part of step three. This problem can be frustrating because people who experience auditory lag are often accused of not paying attention to, or misunderstanding, what was said.

Right hemisphere dominant people are more apt to acquire skills through a demonstration than an explanation. They "tend to master larger concepts first, then prefer to go back and fill in the information gaps" (Freed and Parsons, 1997:54).

In comparison, people who take in information via the left hemisphere "prefer to be told, step by step, how to complete a task, rather than have it demonstrated to them . . . They "digest information piece by piece until there's an 'aha!' and they suddenly get the picture . . . They have a greater tendency to accept and appreciate what they hear and read rather than questioning and thinking independently" (Freed and Parsons, 1997:52).

People who are left hemisphere dominant tend to "go inside of themselves" and take cognizance of their own thoughts and emotions as others communicate. This practice makes them "blind and deaf" to the external world. "They experience an internally focused state wherein their own images, sounds, words, sensations, et cetera provide the most compelling data" (Bodenhammer and Hall, 1997:67).

Left brained people tend to pay attention to *what* other people say, instead of how they say it. They actively input information, usually along a line of inquiry. There seems to be a correlation between the attention paid to language, terms, phrases, and their tendency to be verbal rather than non-verbal (Bodenhammer and Hall, 1997). They may act on the other person's words and overlook the sneer on the person's face that might have put their words in question.

Expression versus Outputting

Left hemisphere outputting (talk) tends to be direct, what some people have called "task-oriented." It also tends to include all information relevant to understanding the message. The left hemisphere focuses attention on the production of linear, grammatically correct language. It emphasizes logic, syntax, and grammar.

The left hemisphere's preoccupation with facts, data, and figures seems to predispose it toward rational thinking. This type of thought is linear and sequential, and is reflected in the linearity of expression (outputting) observed in speech.

The right hemisphere, on the other hand, *expresses* rather than outputting. Its expression is primarily nonverbal through gesture, movement, and facial expression. There has to be some sort of transfer process to move information typically stored as sensory mental images (sounds, feelings, and tastes) to the verbal left hemisphere for translation into words. This transfer time may account for the pauses observed in the outputting of right hemisphere dominant people. The effect of the pauses for translation and transfer can be seen in the relatively slow pace of right brained outputting.

The large amount of data processed by the right hemisphere and its lack of focused attention may explain why right brained people tend to speak in an "around about" or rambling manner. They also tend not to be very concerned with enunciation or the precision of language, which can be observed in their tendency to mumble and use cliché-laden language. If left-brained people talk in straight lines (directly), then right-brained people talk in curved lines or circles (indirectly). They also tend not to pay attention to vocabulary outside of their own technical fields. Right-brained people tend to tell stories packed with context (immediately surrounding the event like what so and so was wearing, who they came with, their mood, etc.), rather than issue the streamlined data-oriented talk associated with left brained people.

The right brain expresses itself in a much less structured way than the left brain. There are often many digressions and intuitive leaps in the communication styles of right hemisphere dominant people. It is also common for right brain output to be presented in the form of metaphors and analogies.

Reading and Influencing

Both reading people and influencing people require the targeted use of both the right and left hemispheres of the brain. Reading people is largely about pattern recognition. It requires the ability to perceive behaviors subtle or gross and associate them with specific circumstances. The range of potential "data" as behaviors can be seen, heard, or felt. The breadth of data that must be observed favors the right hemisphere. The "gill netting" strategy of the right hemisphere is more effective at dealing with these various stimuli than the narrow, targeted observation of the left hemisphere. Not only must "data" be observed; but they must also be processed.

The most critical skill in reading people is sensory acuity. It requires the ability to detect changes in another individual without fixing your attention on a particular act or moment. This is easier said than done. Most people attempt to analyze a salient behavior moments after detecting it. Analysis requires leaving "the scene" as you go inside to derive meaning. Obviously, anything that occurs subsequent to the moment of "departure" is missed.

The objective of observation is to detect patterns of behavior associated with specific situational conditions. The basic questions to be answered are, "What did you see? What did you hear?" These observations must be recorded or noted in the context of specific situational variables. The power of any interpretation is enhanced through the accumulation of repeat themes or patterns in the data. Behaviors that recur under the same circumstances provide the potential for meaningful associations.

Broad awareness is greatly favored over keen focus when observing another person. You want to be generally aware of what the other person does. One of the ways to narrow your focus without narrowing your awareness is to know whether the person is right or left brain dominant, visual, auditory, or kinesthetic. Another way of making the observation process more manageable is to generally know what the probable range of behaviors are in a specific interaction. Such knowledge allows the observer to focus attention on specific variables that are likely to yield the most information during the interaction. For example, you can anticipate or control the introduction of new information in a new proposal, thus giving you the opportunity to note changes in behavior point by point.

The steps in deriving meaning start with identifying behaviors and observing when and how they occur; then associating specific circumstances to observed behaviors. You might note that a person's face becomes flush, and that this seems to occur during moments when important decisions are being made. Later, you might notice skin color changes with a delay in speech; and even later, you might notice color changes just before the person says that she does not have the authority to make a specific decision. After the interaction, you would describe the skin color change in greater detail, and take the aggregate of your data to allow you to conclude that the color changes become evident whenever the person has to make a decision or take a stand.

Two Chips Passing in the Night

The importance of thinking styles (information processing) in negotiations was not evident to me until a negotiation exercise as part of an executive MBA class activity a few years ago. Our class was full of bright, successful high-level managers and executives, but there were some significant thinking style differences among us. We came from backgrounds as diverse as medicine, architecture, and computer chip manufacturing. One Intel manager was particularly interesting. He was one of the youngest people in the class, had an engineering degree, was of European-American descent from the Pacific Northwest, and spoke Japanese. He also sometimes spoke so fast that he slurred his words. He also seemed to make deductions that we often didn't understand – everyone except our statistics professor. After a while, some people in the class started to discount what he had to say. They thought of his speech as random thought generation, and would even tease him about it. In time, I noticed that he typically formulated ideas requiring insights and leaps of logic so far ahead of the class that his comments only made sense to me a couple of days after he had made them. Much of the problem in understanding him came from the fact that he rarely provided enough context for what he was saying. It also became apparent that understanding what he said required translating his words into a mental image and disregarding the order in which he presented thoughts and ideas. Trying to understand what he said was an interesting intellectual exercise, but I didn't want my grade to depend on it. Unfortunately, that's exactly what happened during a class on negotiation. Members of the class were paired up, given case material, and told to negotiate the terms of an agreement in 60 minutes based on the information in fact sheets. At the end of the allotted time, we had to report the terms of our agreement to the class. When the rest of the class realized who my partner was, they gave me "better you than me" looks, snickered, and suggested that they would see me "tomorrow." My partner and I went to a separate classroom, then individually read our fact sheets and formulated our positions. We then began to negotiate and seemed to be at an impasse immediately. He saw the situation so differently than me that I wondered if he had received the right briefing materials. As time slipped away, I became more and more anxious and became frustrated with his position. Then, I remembered what I had learned about his thinking style from observing him in class discussions. I quickly drew a diagram of my perspective of the problem on the whiteboard; he looked at it briefly, then erased and modified part of it. In less than ten minutes we had an agreement. To the amazement of the class, we were one of the first pairs to complete the exercise and our solution was as good as produced by any others.

How is this event related to nonverbal communication? The following thinking and communication styles complicated the negotiations between my colleague and I. First, he thought in pictures; second, as with most people who think in pictures he assumed that I could see the pictures in his mind; and third, the rate of my speech was distracting to him. While I was selecting and presenting my words to guide his thinking process, he was getting bored and using them to make pictures. Once he had made a picture of what he thought was my perspective, he discarded my words. The subtle nuance of my words were not being interpreted in the way that I hoped because he was making pictures from my words and comparing his understanding of my view to the one he saw in his mind. A "well-articulated" picture, once created, is difficult to modify solely using words. The picture keeps reappearing. You have probably experienced this phenomenon if you have ever seen the classic illusion that from one perspective is an unattractive, old witch, and from the other, is a young, elegant woman. Even when someone points out the image that you didn't see initially, you have great difficulty continuing to see anything but the original image. Not only was it difficult for him to 'see' my perspective, but he was also bored to tears with my attempts to explain it to him because I spoke too slowly. His mind was racing ahead of me and he had difficulty concentrating on what I was saying. Once I drew a picture, he and I could be assured that we were talking about the same thing. He was no longer dependent upon verbal communication and was free to process as fast as he wanted.

Nonverbal communication includes thinking styles, speech patterns, and gesticulation. Some people think like a MacIntosh user. They use icons (pictures) to direct their computer's (mind's) actions. Others input and output using DOS. DOS inputting and outputting is slower, more linear, and more unforgiving in terms of inputting grammar and sequence than a MacIntosh operating system. When a "Mac thinker" and a "DOS thinker" interact, there are bound to be problems with speed and comprehension.

Nonverbals Matter

Meaning in face-to-face interactions is primarily determined by nonverbal behavior. Mehrabian (1972) claimed that an average of 55 percent of nonverbal communication comes from facial cues and 38 percent come from vocal cues. People from all walks of life are starting to realize that nonverbal behaviors (nonverbals) matter. Almost everybody knows that how you said what you said is often more important than what you said. For example, when Clint Eastwood says, "Make my day" or a teenager says "whatever," it is the nonverbal part of the message that tells the listener that he or she is being threatened or their ideas are being dismissed.

Poker players, politicians, salespeople, lawyers, physicians and anyone who interacts with people to either get or give information can benefit from the systematic use of nonverbal behavior. How we communicate with our eyes, voice, body and breathing greatly affects whether we are successful or not in these endeavors. Both imparting and obtaining information are affected by nonverbal behavior. For example, skilled family practitioners are very capable of seeing the symptoms of ailments, but often do not engage patients well enough to get really good family histories. This deficiency is partially a function of time, but it is also all too often related to ineffective bedside manner. Even the family practitioners that have gotten a good family history often complain about the difficulty in convincing a patient to diligently follow a treatment regime. Being able to obtain information requires the ability to ask questions in ways that make it easy for people to retrieve and present information. On the other hand, being able to secure a client's commitment requires the ability to influence behavior. Having someone's attention in a clinic or hospital setting does not have much to do with securing compliance. The more a lawyer, physician, architect or even an electrician understands about how his client or patient listens and understands things, the more effectively he or she can influence their behavior.

In the realm of negotiation, the effective use of nonverbals can be the difference between a brief, efficient negotiation and one that is protracted and hostile. Mediators and negotiators are starting to realize that nonverbal behavior can have profound implications for negotiations. The speed of finding common ground, the amount of conflict experienced, and the prospects for follow-through on agreements are all directly related to the nonverbal dimensions of negotiations.

A variety of professionals from the police to lawyers and negotiators are using nonverbal behavior to detect deception. People have discovered that liars tend to avoid eye contact, that their facial muscles tighten when they lie, and that many have difficulty finding words. Until fairly recently, lie detector machines were considered the best detectors of deception. These machines, in fact, measure a limited number of stress-related (physiological) nonverbal behaviors and associate them with deception. While the reliability of a lie detector may be arguable, stress-related nonverbal behaviors are clearly associated with deception. Human experts on deception, like Paul Ekman, have demonstrated a remarkable ability to identify deception using nonverbal cues.

The Best Nonverbals are Reflexes

Nonverbal behavior is present in all face-to-face or "ear-to ear" communications. "We cannot *not* send nonverbal messages." Attentive people can read our bodies. The way we breathe, the way we move, the way we talk, and our choice of words all reflect what we are focusing on and what our minds are doing at any given time.

Most people mistakenly equate body language with nonverbal behavior. Body language is actually a subset of nonverbal communication; it is primarily about voluntary action. Postures and gestures tend to be voluntary. That is to say, they are the result of conscious choices. We choose to recline, to move forward, and to cross our arms. Anything you choose to do, you can choose not to do for purposes of deception. That's why experts in nonverbal behavior pay attention to habitual and automatic reactions like facial gestures, physiological changes, and changes in voice characteristics. These reactions are a "gold mine" of information.

Automatic responses to situations (stimuli) are interesting because they reveal what is going on deep inside the person(s) in front of us. Very few people can disguise their automatic responses to stimuli. In fact, even those few people who have great control of automatic responses do so through careful preparation. In most cases, they actively control their physiology, especially their breathing, *before* they are exposed to a stimulus thereby reducing their range of automatic responses. In other words, they prevent themselves from getting excited; so when surprised, they react much like anyone else.

Automatic actions are generally involuntary and are typically controlled by the autonomic nervous system. They are the nonverbals of most interest for reading people. The autonomic nervous system (ANS) controls our breathing rate, skin color, pupil dilation, and perspiration, among other things. Lie detector technology presents readings associated with this part of our nervous system to a technician who interprets specific recorded changes in the subject's physiology as attempts at deception.

The speed of the ANS's response to stimuli has led researchers to conclude that these virtually automatic responses to situations (stimuli) are primarily unconscious. Our reactions are so fast that we do not have time to think about our actions; we obviously just react. We recognize a threat (a mental activity), and then act. Once we perceive danger, our nervous system supplies us with the energy to confront the threat (fight) or run away from it (flight).

The fact that our nervous systems are designed to respond to pain and pleasure is central to reading people's responses to events and actions. We automatically react to our experience or anticipation of pain or pleasure, and those responses are registered as emotions. Emotions are so important to our survival that we even have pain and pleasure centers in our brains (Pierce, 1994). When the pain center is stimulated, the fight or flight response is activated; whereas, stimulation of the pleasure center prompts a relaxation response.

Each emotion seems to have unique physiological responses. For example, anxiety leads to increases in systolic blood pressure, anger increases diastolic blood pressure; and fear causes the skin to pale, while anger causes the skin to become flush. Physiological responses to emotion can be cardiovascular, muscular-skeletal, thermoregulatory, respiratory, gastrointestinal, urinary, and reproductive (Goleman, 1995). Reading people in "real-time" requires knowing the general physiological expressions of emotion.

Even though standard signs of emotion are universal, the expression of emotions in individuals can vary. For example anger generally involves turning red, but for some people different parts of their bodies may change color before their faces do. Accurately and precisely interpreting people's nonverbal behavior requires an appreciation of the unique patterns of the individual being observed.

Too Quick to Lie

The type of nonverbal communication addressed in succeeding chapters is more reliable than body language because it bypasses our conscious mind. Its value lies in the fact that goals have an emotional charge and that emotions register on people's faces and bodies. Professional poker players and elite negotiators understand how important this form of nonverbal communication can be because of its immediacy and directness. Emotional responses are automatic responses, so they cannot easily be disguised and consequently are rich in information. Anytime a negotiator has a chance to consciously think about an action, he has the opportunity to disguise his true motives and intentions. "Automatic" responses preclude that opportunity; thus they are very reliable indicators of true feelings and thoughts.

Emotional responses can be either fast or slow depending on the stimulus. In a slow process, sense organs (eyes, ears, nose, skin) transmit signals to the thalamus and the signals are passed on to the neocortex ("thinking cap") where they are put together into objects we recognize. The neocortex sorts the signals for meanings as it recognizes what each object is and what its presence means. It then sends signals to the limbic brain, and from there, responses radiate throughout the body (Goleman, 1995).

The almost instantaneous quality of the fast process is the basis for assessing the desirability of an action or proposal in real-time. The amygdala, a seahorse-shaped organ located just above the brainstem, is essential to this fast process because of its location and function. The physiology of the process validates emphasizing these nonverbal patterns over traditional body language.

The speed of the fast reaction comes from the fact that sensory signals branch out and take a short and direct path from the thalamus to the amygdala, while other signals in the slow process travel along the longer path to the cortex. The amygdala determines the emotional significance of events; and when it associates emotional intensity with a stimulus, it initiates rapid and visible changes in body chemistry. Direct inputs from the senses and a short pathway allow the amygdala to start a response *before* signals are fully registered by our thinking brain. In other words, the amygdala facilitates emotional reactions before we have fully understood what is happening. A well-tuned response to a stimulus (precision) is sacrificed for speed. The body, in essence, chooses to be "better safe than sorry." Additionally, the amygdala can house memories, emotional impressions and response behaviors that are triggered without our conscious control because "the shortcut from thalamus to amygdala completely bypasses the neocortex" (Goleman, 1995:18).

The amygdala has been called our "emotional sentinel." It scans our experience for answers to simple questions. "Is this something I hate?" "Is this something that hurts me?" "Is this something I fear?" If the answer is "yes" to any of these questions, the body's fight or flight mechanism is activated and the body reacts accordingly. In most cases (sometimes we freeze), we become more alert and we get a burst of energy to deal with the threat. In short, the amygdala activates reflexes away from pain and toward pleasure.

Our reflex responses are extraordinarily fast because we are biologically programmed to process very little information before we act. We react to fragments of information – often just shapes, movements, or symbols. These fragments can be the suggestive shape of something coiled in a corner, a slithering movement, or an unexpected move by someone unknown to us. Once interpreted as a threat, the body immediately releases a dose of adrenalin that fuels a vigorous reaction.

Responses that allow for the appraisal of a situation (involve thinking) are very slow compared to these reflex responses. Action, in the slow process, is preceded by a conscious thought process based on an assessment of the pain or pleasure associated with a stimulus (action, proposal or gesture). We generally appraise the situation according to how well a stimulus fits our goals (Lazarus, 1991). Our goals, however, tend to be culturally defined. In other words, our education, social background, and family strongly influence our ideas about what is desirable. Decision making is ultimately an effort to find the choice that most effectively satisfies our values (Bleiker, 1986).

"Tells" Betray Values

The connection between the brain and body can be exploited when assessing someone's values. Since values always have an emotional charge, they are expressed in the body. This means that when someone experiences something pleasurable, their body exhibits signs of pleasure. Similarly, unpleasant thoughts and feelings from exposure to something threatening are expressed in the body as signs of distress, fear, and anxiety. Amazingly, your physiology can even change significantly in response to a vivid thought *without* the presence of a stimulus.

Nonverbal behavior reveals much more than intention and motivation. It can also indirectly reveal people's values. The brain and the body are connected in such a way that reading the body at the right time can give you important information about someone's general preferences for processes (communication and decision making) and outcomes. For example, it is possible to know whether they generally emphasize facts, form, or feelings, as well as, their preference for logic, procedure or emotional display by observing body posture and listening to diction and voice characteristics such as pitch.

In summary, an individual's values are on display as physiological "tells" in response to particular situations. A proposal or action consistent with an individual's values may prompt his or her pupils to dilate, facial muscles to relax, or even a smile. Hearing, seeing or even envisioning something desirable often produces the physiology of relaxation or tension. Responses to things that repel people are often stronger and easier to observe than those that produce pleasure. Individuals may recoil, frown, or even stop breathing momentarily. Information about their likes and dislikes are constantly available to you – if you pay attention to what their bodies are saying. People can control what they say verbally, but they can't control what their bodies say.

The Signposts: Eyes, Voice, Body, and Breathing

Nonverbal behavior can be organized into four major areas: eyes, voice, body, and breathing. Classical body language mainly emphasizes one of these areas – the body including the head and face. Unfortunately, it also emphasizes a catalog of behaviors each having an assigned meaning like crossed legs closed toward another person indicating that a person is closed to another person's ideas, or shoulders thrown back indicating pride or a demonstration of power. There are two problems with these notions of "body language:" first, the misconception that body language and nonverbal behavior are synonymous. Second, body language tends to disregard both context and idiosyncratic behavior. There is no doubt that there is a high correlation between some "body language" and certain interpretations, but the strategic use of nonverbal behavior requires that we pay attention to the context in which things occur and the individual's "normal" behavior. People putting their hands to their mouths may actually be trying to conceal something or disapproval, but it is difficult to know for sure without knowing something about the situation. One way to do this is to construct a baseline of person's behaviors. The baseline establishes his or her normal behaviors associated with reticence, excitement, and the delivery of facts. This is relatively easy to do in a negotiation because there is generally a round of small talk in which people try to break the ice and get to know each other.

The better we know the "game" or the structure of the interaction, the more we can pay attention to nonverbal factors. Thinking about a specific move and our own needs too much often distracts us from critical cues. Just as a poker player cannot focus on reading "tells" until he or she has learned the rules of the game, negotiators need to know the negotiation ritual before trying to attend to nonverbal behavior. Otherwise, they will be inundated by information and be unable to make sense of it. Put another way, an actor cannot refine her performance until she knows her character and the script intimately. Negotiators also have to know themselves and the nature of the ritual before being able to focus attention externally.

Eye behavior can be very revealing. It can tell us how a person is using his or her brain at any particular time. It can also reveal what is important to a person or give us cues about what has captured their attention. Eye avoidance behavior can also suggest the presence of a guilty conscience or, in a poker game, an effort to set a trap as in the story previously discussed.

Professional poker player, Mike Caro, reveals the importance of eye behavior at critical times in the following comment, "When a player has a really strong hand, they have one almost universal tendency. As the action approaches them, they don't want to discourage anybody from betting, so . . . they look away. Sometimes their eyes [but not their heads] even turn back toward the action. That's a dead give away that they are ready to pounce."

Blinking, pupil dilation and tearing are all eye behaviors that can have meaning in social interactions. While blinking can be voluntary, it can also be involuntary as when someone is aroused. It can also be present when someone is having difficulty trying to "see" something. Pupils dilate involuntarily when we are aroused as when we are excited, or experience fear or anger. Tears are also produced involuntarily. They reveal intense emotional involvement, but can be associated with distress, sadness, relief, certain forms of enjoyment, or uncontrolled laughter.

"Voice" refers to everything involved in speech other than the words themselves. Tone, pitch, volume, and speech rate all fall into this category. "Changes in voice produced by emotion are not easy to conceal" (Ekman, 1992:93). Tension and stress are often revealed in changes of pitch. The speed of speech also indirectly tells us something about how a person is processing information and their general preferences.

The body, in our categories, includes the face. Faces reveal a great deal of information about emotions. Some facial expressions associated with emotions are universal including: fear, anger, disgust, sadness, and distress regardless of age, sex, color or culture (Ekman, 1992). The face can show which emotion is being felt, the presence of more than one emotion, and the strength of an emotion. Some facial expressions can be controlled, others can't. More interestingly, emotions often "leak," that is, escape concealment and register on the face for very brief, almost imperceptible periods averaging 1/25 of a second (Ekman, 2001).

The face reveals internal activity through color changes like blushing and blanching. Sweating also occurs around the face and can be an indication of stress or anxiety.

The body includes posture, gestures, and proxemics. A great deal can be learned from the observation of a person's body in an interaction. For example, the tilt of a person's head can reveal how they are processing information and their distribution of weight on their feet is an indication of their perceptive ability in the moment.

The autonomic nervous system (ANS) is particularly revealing about a person's internal state because it produces noticeable changes in the body associated with emotional arousal. Psychologists studying lie detection tend to focus on breathing patterns, the frequency of swallowing, and the amount of sweating. This seems a little limited. The ANS mediates many other important physiological functions, especially a person's heart and breathing rate. The most conspicuous signs of ANS activity are blanching, blushing, and breathing rate.

Breathing patterns are the most important aspects of nonverbal behavior because they directly affect what you do with your voice and body. They also respond unconsciously and within micro-seconds to what is perceived by your sensory organs, especially your eyes. Humans also often unconsciously react to other people's breathing patterns. For example, the speaker who is so tense that his voice squeaks and cracks will often make you audience anxious. Although you are reacting to the stress in his voice, his voice is the by-product of ineffective breathing.

Breathing patterns can make or break people; just ask Al Gore. His shallow breathing made him look stiff, and his untimely sighs led the press to paint an unflattering impression of him. You can't have charisma if your breathing makes you look stiff. If words were the determining factors in people's evaluations of presidential debates Gore might be president today. It seems fair to say that words were not nearly as important as nonverbal messages in the presidential debates of 1960 (Nixon-Kennedy), 1984 (Dukakis-Bush), and 2000 (Bush-Gore).

Poker players and negotiators are not oblivious to the actions of the ANS. Caro (2001) reveals the value of appreciating the ANS in the following comments about how poker players respond to an exceptional hand. "Very frequently you can hear the extra breathing stimulated by the monster hand. The breath quickens. Never call that bet because that player has a strong hand."

It's a Competitive Game

Many social interactions such as business meetings, cocktail parties, negotiations, are games. All games, are designed to make optimal performance possible by having rules that require learning skills, developing goals, and obtaining and using feedback. Persuasion, whether conducted in the context of negotiations, sales, or courtroom battle is a competitive game. In these games, "the participant must stretch her skills to meet the challenge provided by the skills of the opponents" (Csiksezentmihalyi, 1990:72).

The ability to read nonverbal behavior in real-time is challenging, but well worth the effort. While negotiations and courtroom battles are really complex, they like other rituals, involve rules and fairly predictable events and issues. As in any game, knowledge of the rules, procedures, and important situations is critical before you can interpret another person's nonverbal communication or use your nonverbals to influence them.

When you know the rules of the game and typical behavior patterns, you have the basis for reading the meaning of behaviors. Knowing the rules of nonverbal behavior adds a whole new dimension to games. For example, knowing that it is relatively easy to avoid talking about a thought or feeling, but almost impossible to *hide* an important thought or feeling creates new opportunities for information gathering.

The stress of the situation that produces a thought or feeling, our efforts to hide it from others, and the power of associated emotions all visibly affect our behavior. A careful observer notes changes in how we breathe, move, or talk. In fact, it is not really that difficult to identify salient behaviors because many people perform them habitually when they find themselves in stressful situations. For example, an attorney/mediator who was trying to figure out my position in a prospective deal – without giving away his own, revealed a nervous habit that I hadn't noticed in years of interacting with him. As he realized that he was going to have to tell me more than he wanted to, he became frustrated, stopped breathing for a split second and then quickly pushed his shirtsleeve up from his wrist with a twisting movement. I was unaware of this behavior until I watched him carefully and realized that he had exhibited the same pattern of behavior in other stressful situations. This man's "tell" can be used to effectively to manipulate him because it reveals when he is off balance and being forced to make an adjustment that he hasn't thought through. Aggressive, win-lose negotiators take advantage of the moments of indecision that his behavior signifies. Indecision and confusion are seen as opportunities to maneuver opponents into accepting deals on their terms. "Predators" rarely miss such obvious nonverbal cues because they are always watching you and trying to figure you out.

Influence is Nonverbal

The most persuasive people don't rely on words to influence you – they use their bodies – and if they are really skilled, they use yours. They know that words are less than 30 percent of the message and that nonverbal behavior has the greatest influence on the listener. Until recently people believed that nonverbal communication was intentional communication witnessed by another person. Now many people believe that it includes unintentional nonverbal behavior including: visual, vocal, and invisible communication systems such as touch, smell, and the use of time (Leathers, 1992).

The potential for using nonverbal behavior can be used as a persuasive tool because personal motives for changing beliefs and behaviors are rooted in values. Using nonverbal behavior to read and prioritize values, and gauge responses to proposals can greatly improve a person's persuasive power. The logic underlying this statement works this way. People are motivated by their need to avoid pain or gain pleasure and they are also inclined to associate either pain or pleasure to proposals, ideas, or events. Since the perception of pain and pleasure creates perceptible physiological changes an astute observer can gauge the emotional appeal of a proposal, idea, or event based on perceived changes in a listener-perceiver's physiology. Not only can a person read another person's reaction to a proposal, but he or she should also be able to use a similar strategy to discern value preferences and create an argument that appeals to them by associating pleasure with an offer, or pain with an alternative.

The physiology associated with emotions is well-established (Howard, 1994). For example, we can correlate loss of blood in the face, elevated heart rate, and cold skin to fear, and pupil dilation, a quickening heart rate and increased muscle tone to arousal. A range of emotions has been correlated with easily observed physiological changes.

The ability to assess information-processing style using physiological indicators is also well-documented (Herrmann, 1985; Grinder, 1991). Field research has made it possible to correlate behavioral cues with thinking and communication styles (Bretto, 1988; Grinder, 1991). We now can identify gross – and micro-movements that inform us of which sensory channel is most accessible thinking processes and value preferences in real-time. Values are discernible because they always have an emotional charge; and emotions are visceral – they have physiological markers.

The fact that values have an emotional charge and that people generally associate pain or pleasure with situations makes it possible to monitor how well a presentation, offer, or action is being received in the moment. Taking advantage of the two-way exchange of nonverbal communication in a negotiation makes it possible to make real-time adjustments during a negotiation.

Structure Simplifies Reading

We are constantly trying to influence the people around us. Sometimes our efforts to influence each other are ritualistic or formal as in an episode of negotiation, an employment interview, or a political speech, and at other times, they are informal and spontaneous. The more predictable the interaction, the easier it is to use nonverbal behavior strategically. Similarly, the more ritualistic or structured the situation, the easier it is to manage. A structured situation reduces the range of action-reaction possibilities making it easier to focus on specific actions and outcomes. It also makes it possible to choreograph interactions. Now you know one of the reasons why sales managers at car dealerships want you to come to their offices.

Structured situations also make it easier to observe and understand nonverbal behavior because there are fewer variables to interpret; fewer variables and fewer possible meanings. They also make nonverbal behavior easier to understand, so nonverbals will be presented in the context of specific situations.

Top performers in sales, negotiations, and courtrooms pay attention to the nonverbal cues of others and are skilled at orchestrating their own. Being systematic about what to look for and how to deliver the right message at the right time is the difference between the best and the rest. Understanding nonverbal behavior and using it systematically is what makes it possible to effectively answer the following questions.

- ❏ How do I know when somebody is ready to make a deal?
- ❏ How do I know when someone is about to concede a point?
- ❏ How do I know when he or she finds me, or my proposal, appealing?
- ❏ How do I assess their position?

The best negotiators and poker players know the answers to these questions by "reading you." They take advantage of what they are seeing and hearing to predict what others are likely to do, and when. Top-notch con men, poker players, and salespeople rely on their knowledge of their respective "games" to assess their position and the range of moves of others. They then focus on the "tells" of the other "players" to select and time their moves. A "tell" is a nonverbal signal that reveals the position or intention of another person. For example, a skilled poker player will observe your efforts to try to fool him about the strength of your hand by paying close attention to the way you manage your body, what you say, and your breathing. Mike Caro (a professional poker player) illustrates the point this way, "a lot of people, especially weak players manifest one single thing over and over. They act weak when they have strong hands and they act strong when they have weak hands. A weak player may have a little bit [of] extra emphasis at the end of his bet, and that emphasis means to me that he needs to convince me that he's strong. So what is he? He's weak." A few of important points can be inferred from Caro's observation: you have to pay attention to the behaviors of the person in front of you; 2) you have to consider the context in which a behavior occurs; and finally, 3) people's behavior is habitual.

Even the most subtle and secretive people offer "tells" to others – they can't help it. The fact is that "the things we think, the things we want, we can do them or not do them, but we can't hide them" (Mamet, 1987). Poker and negotiations are different "games," but the difference between good "players" and the best in both fields lie in the ability to manage and read nonverbal behavior. Each game makes different demands. Poker players and con men "live and die" by their ability to read and manage "tells." Similarly, elite negotiators and mediators improve their prospects for agreement by reading "tells."

Reading people's behaviors as they play cards is relatively simple compared to doing it during a negotiation. The pace of a card game is relatively slow and there is plenty of time to observe others thinking and acting. Additionally, there are fewer distractions and fewer variables to consider in cards. The players all know that the cards in their hands largely determine their tactics and they all have to periodically assess the quality of their hands vis-à-vis those of others.

While poker and negotiations are different from each other, they share some critical features. They both involve more than one person competing for a limited resource, interdependent moves, and action-reaction sequences. Moves made by others and assessments of our position and options have the potential to elicit emotional responses in both poker and negotiations. Poker players and negotiators both need real-time information to make tactical decisions. They both know emotions are hard to hide, and therefore count on being able to read the emotional responses of others to assess their relative positions. For the poker player, opportunity and ability to read others, are facilitated by knowledge of the cards in play and the probabilities of certain hands occurring.

When the stakes are high enough, fear or excitement will be present, and nonverbal cues will be conspicuous. Emotional energy produces physical movement; and that movement can be either large or subtle. Some people change their posture or fidget. More experienced "players" (many people consider most competitive interactions as games) react more subtly, but even they have difficulty not reflecting pain or pleasure on their faces. Even a master will reveal changes in physiology in the way he or she breathes. Breathing patterns, skin color changes, muscle tension, perspiration and gaze behavior are all nonverbal cues can be read relative to the situation in which they occur.

The Nonverbals of Decision Making

Understanding how people make decisions makes it possible to see how people's nonverbal behaviors can be used to frame offers and also to gauge reactions to offers. Negotiators, politicians, service providers, and salespeople all engage people to make decisions favorable to them. They all face the same challenge: getting people to associate pleasure with their proposals. This process is necessary because decision making is always an attempt to maximize the satisfaction of personal values. Contrary to conventional thinking, decision-making really is emotional – even supposedly objective decision making. There is mounting evidence that the old sales cliché that people "buy emotionally and justify rationally" is actually true. It appears that we use rational thought to assess the weight of facts, but we assign weight to those facts based on our individual value system. The fact that the body's reactions to pain and pleasure are spontaneous and reflexive (basically uncontrollable), makes it both an effective and reliable for gauging the effect of a message, situation or proposal. There is no need for sophisticated equipment to read people's nonverbal reactions; the signs of pleasure and pain are conspicuous. You just need to know what to look for, and have a method for assessing data.

Nonverbal behavior from now on will refer to behaviors associated with the speaker-sender or listener-perceiver's eyes, voice, body, and breathing patterns. We observe, what is happening inside another person by looking at external physiological (nonverbal behavior) indicators. We can use this information coupled with knowledge of another set of physio-psychological reactions called "fixed-action patterns" to influence people nonverbally. Fixed-action patterns are patterns of behavior that occur in the same way and in the same order whenever people are exposed to a specific stimulus. All animals seem to exhibit their own fixed action patterns. So-called "horse whisperers" use the automatic nature of the fixed-action patterns of horses to secure compliance without using physical force. They understand the psychology of horses and the triggers (nonverbal cues) that induce specific patterns of behavior. They then use these to put the horse in a position where it willingly chooses to submit to them.

Humans also have automatic fixed-action patterns (Cialdini, 1984); and anyone using their nonverbal triggers (nonverbal) strategically can influence their behavior. The seven keys to influence presented in this book are designed around these triggers. Incidentally, many magicians use fixed action patterns to do magic. They know how your mind works and how to use their bodies to affect your perception of events so that you believe that the impossible has occurred.

Buying is Value-Driven

There is a cliché that people buy emotionally and justify their decisions rationally. It's true. Recent PET scan studies of decision-making have verified it. As Dr. Dean Shibata, assistant professor of radiology at the University of Washington says, "Our imaging research supports the idea that every time you have to make choices in your personal life, you need to 'feel' the projected emotional outcome of each choice – subconsciously or intuitively." In other words, we use emotions in personal decision making; although they tend to be applied to decision making as values (standards with emotional charge). In fact, Dr. Hans Bleiker, an expert in decision-making, asserts that all decision making is an effort to satisfy our values as much as possible. Values are personal definitions of pain and pleasure in terms of desirable outcomes and how things ought to be done.

Values are the *evalu*ation criteria we use to make decisions; and all values have an emotional charge. Put simply, we experience values in our bodies. When values are satisfied, we experience pleasure; and when they are violated, we experience pain. We find pleasure in actions and situations that enable us to achieve desirable outcomes. Conversely, the prospects for an undesirable outcome produce anxiety, fear, or discomfort.

The way our brains are configured also appears to influence our values. Our brains are composed of two specialized hemispheres. For example, the left hemisphere facilitates talk and language recognition, while the right hemisphere facilitates singing and harmony. Although we rely on both the hemispheres of our brains to get through our daily activities, we tend to favor one side of the brain. Interestingly, that preference is reflected in our values. "Left-brained" people (someone with a preference for the left hemisphere) are more schedule and task-oriented than right-brained people (Grinder, 1999). The frustration that American negotiators have about "not getting down to business" fast enough when negotiating in Mexico the result of two sets of values about the use of time colliding. American culture's values about time are consistent with left-brain dominance. Mexican cultural norms, on the other hand, are more reflective of right-brained dominance. They place emphasis on establishing favorable interpersonal relationships before addressing tasks like negotiating a deal. In this case, the differences in brain dominance are manifested in the way these two cultures organize time and prioritize tasks – important nonverbal behaviors. Differences in values are almost always evident in nonverbal behaviors like deference, demeanor, and proxemics.

Values affect decision making in several important ways. They assist us in determining the nature of a problem by telling us what is important in a specific situation. Values fix our attention on specific aspects of a situation at the expense of others. They basically frame situations for us.

Values also affect perception, or the conscious acknowledgement of sensed stimuli. They influence what our brains filter out from sensory inputs. We see, hear, and feel far too much "data" for our conscious minds to process. Values, bundled into cultures, instruct the brain about what to filter out so we can consciously work with a manageable amount of inputs (theoretically five plus or minus two). Mature members of a culture demonstrate their knowledge of that culture by paying attention to the things the culture deems important.

Values operate on yet another level of decision-making. They define and prioritize acceptable solutions to problems. People evaluate options by examining how well those options satisfy their values. Actually, solutions that do not satisfy basic values are not considered feasible. Interestingly, extensive empirical research on associations between brain dominance and specific behaviors and preferences has been conducted in recent years (Meister Vitale, 1982; Herrmann, 1995). We now know that specific values, skills, and modes of information processing are correlated with the right and left hemispheres of the brain. For example, logic, order, sequence and locating details and facts are associated with left hemisphere dominance. Values and preferences associated with the right hemisphere include flexibility, intuition, and spontaneity, and pattern recognition. Careful observation of people's nonverbal behavior reveals their brain dominance, thereby giving us insights about preferences and ways to deliver information for maximum impact.

Everybody's decisions are guided by his or her values. If this weren't true, con men wouldn't be able to ply their trade. The importance of values in con games is evident in a scene from the 1987 movie "House of Games" in which a con man (confidence man) illustrates the "short con" for a psychologist. He explains that a con man places his confidence in you and counts on you to reciprocate by placing your confidence in him. The scene illustrating the short con shows the con man manipulating a soldier to offer him money by striking up a conversation as the soldier waits at a Western Union station for money to be wired to him. The con man establishes rapport with the soldier then finds out why he needs the money; the con man then offers to lend the soldier the money he needs to catch the bus back to the base, if his money arrives first. The con man places his confidence in the soldier by telling him that he can mail him back the money when he gets to his base. Surprisingly, when the soldier's money arrives first, the soldier insists on offering him some money. The con man later says, "I give that guy my confidence, I ask him for help and what he gets is he feels like he's a good man [by helping me]." This con relied on the fact that people *value* feeling good about themselves by helping someone who they think deserves it.

The Choreography of Influence

Asserting influence, whether in one-way or two-way transactions, involves choreography. One-way interactions are simple, whereas two-way dynamic interactions are complex because they involve cause and effect, then cycles of action and reaction. In simple applications the speaker-sender is the initiator or the cause and the effect is the intended objective. The speaker-sender anticipates and controls situational factors and acts toward achieving a clear objective. Speaker-senders need to understand the physical space in which they will act as well as the attitudes and interests of the target audience. They depend on their ability to control the sound and ambiance of the location, visuals including the backdrop, and even the pacing of the event. The roles of the participants are well-known and circumscribed in one-way transactions. The choreographer determines what the message is to be, and what the audience will pay attention to consciously and most importantly, unconsciously. Timing and execution then become the critical elements of the performance. Effective execution by the speaker-sender requires delivering messages in the right location and with the appropriate words, posture, gesture, and voice.

Simple applications are one-way communications. The audience is passive and receives a message that influences it, as in current political campaign advertising and marketing. A goal is set, a target audience is selected, and an encounter is planned and orchestrated. The positioning of the audience (whether in front of a TV monitor or in the sales manager's at the dealership) is determined in advance. The amount of light, whether it is artificial or natural, sight lines, fields of vision, furnishings, color schemes, and the use of space are all considered to grab "eyeballs" and produce the desired effect. Nowadays, backdrops are carefully considered, the wardrobe of the speaker, and the posture and movement of the speaker or spokesperson.

Current one-way efforts to influence others can be very sophisticated. Political campaigns, for example, are highly orchestrated for television coverage and campaign ads. The most conspicuous example of the lengths that campaigns are willing to go to was the "Mission Accomplished" video of President Bush. This was clearly an effort to create the impression of a powerful, experienced warrior leader.

The backdrop was a pre-positioned aircraft carrier (it had to be turned around to get the right view for the camera), the Abraham Lincoln. The president in full flight gear landed a jet fighter on the deck after a very short flight. The president lands the plane and emerges in his flight outfit to be surrounded by adoring troops enthralled by their overwhelming victory over the Iraqis. He walks to his mark and announces, "Mission accomplished!" In the background is a banner prominently displaying the same statement. This was an expensive commercial, but it was critical to implanting the idea of a warrior president, not just a warrior – a Top Gun. The kind of leader that the people in Middle America are assured will keep them safe from terrorism.

The most common example of this choreography can be seen in the performance of stage magicians. They take advantage of the fact that they know what you can perceive and how you are likely to perceive it. They also know when to direct your attention away from what is actually occurring in front of you.

Two-way transactions are far more complex than the one-way transactions. Salespeople, police officers, physicians, attorneys, and negotiators engage in these types of interactions daily in the pursuit of their goals. Two-way transactions potentially involve all of the elements of a one-way transaction, but are complicated by the fact that the listener-perceiver can and does act in response to the speaker-sender's actions. The listener-perceiver is active not passive, as in a simple application. The first challenge is get his or her attention. Once you have it, you have to know what people pay attention to consciously and unconsciously, as well as, how to hold conscious attention.

Getting and building rapport are critical to asserting influence in two-way interactions. They are about establishing relationships and then guiding attention and the formation of impressions. Understanding and making use of fixed action patterns is critical to efficiency and effectiveness in two-way interactions. Skilled speaker-senders manage their own nonverbal behavior to influence listener-perceivers in dynamic, two-way interactions.

The highest level of influence is accomplished in a give and take dynamic. This requires the ability to perceive the nonverbal behavior of the other person, and almost instantaneously respond with intentional nonverbal behavior of your own that moves them in a direction favorable to your interests. Some people are naturally remarkably adept at this, but they usually are not detail people. Too much attention to detail, and you lose contact with the moment.

There seems to be an organic limitation on people's ability to manage two-way transactions. It is not possible to be totally open to perception and analyze a situation at the same time. Effective influence in two-way transactions requires relaxation. Relaxation makes it possible to achieve high levels of perception and produce efficient responses.

Influence in a two-way transaction is tactically effective, but not necessarily strategically effective. The broad awareness of the right brain facilitates reactions to concrete, immediate environmental factors. Strategic thinking, however, involves the assessment of abstractions, consideration of the current situation relative to the future or the past, and analysis all of which require the involvement of the left brain. There is a tension between staying in the moment (being tactical) and anticipating reactions or consequences (strategic thinking).

The Human Stress Response

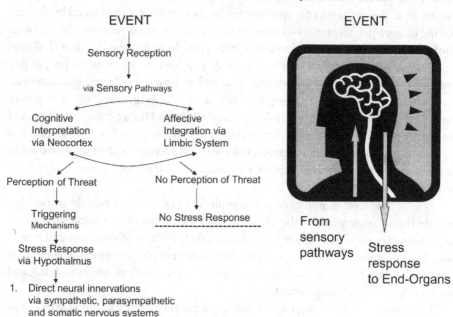

EVENT

↓

Sensory Reception

↓

via Sensory Pathways

Cognitive
Interpretation
via Neocortex

Affective
Integration via
Limbic System

Perception of Threat

No Perception of Threat

↓

Triggering
Mechanisms

No Stress Response

↓

Stress Response
via Hypothalmus

↓

1. Direct neural innervations
    via sympathetic, parasympathetic
    and somatic nervous systems
2. "Fight-Flight Response
3. General Adaptation Syndrome

↓

End-Organ

EVENT

From
sensory
pathways

Stress
response
to End-Organs

THE NERVOUS SYSTEM

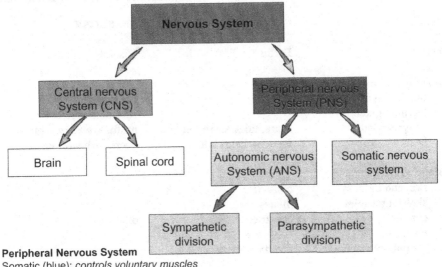

Peripheral Nervous System
Somatic (blue): *controls voluntary muscles*
Autonomic (red): *controls involuntary muscles*
Sympathetic: *expends energy*
Parasympathetic: *conserves energy*

Table 1. Responses of End Organs to Autonomic Nervous System Impulses

	SNS (gas)	PNS (brake)
Function	CATABOLISM	ANABOLISM
Activity	Diffuse	Discrete
Specific actions		
pupil of eye	dilates	constricts
lacrimal gland	------	stimulates secretion
salivary glands	spare, thick secretion	profuse, watery secretion
heart	increase heart rate	decrease heart rate
Blood vessels		
skin and mucosa	constricts	
skeletal muscles	dilates	
cerebral	constricts	dilates
renal	constricts	
abdominal viscera	mostly constricts	
Lungs: bronchial tubes	dilates	constricts
Sweat glands	stimulates	constricts
GI tract	inhibits digestion decreases peristalsis and tone	increased digestion increases peristalsis and tone
Kidney	decreases output of urine	

Seven Keys to Influence

Every thought or feeling we have is not necessarily registered as a bodily sensation. Every emotion is, however registered; and emotions are involved in thinking and feeling. Research has clearly established that the brain (mind) and body are connected and that emotions go from the mind/brain to the body and back, in many situations.

The word emotion literally means "movement out" in Latin. Internal physiological changes are actually moving out to be seen by others. Emotions are biologically determined processes that operate automatically; and in spite of individual and cultural variation are expressed are fairly stereotypically.

Rational thought does not require bodily sensation unless problems become very complex or complicated. However, when attention or working memory is taxed by the scope or depth of a problem our bodies become engaged to streamline our decision making. Damasio (1994) calls this the "somatic marker" process. He explains that we experience an automated alarm signal that alerts us to the danger ahead for choosing an option that leads to a particular undesirable outcome. "The signal protects you from future losses and simplifies decision making by reducing the number of alternatives to choose among" (Damasio, 1994:173).

The process works by using feelings generated by social (secondary) emotions to eliminate possible choices. Social emotions include embarrassment, jealousy, guilt or pride. When these emotions are registered on the body during this type of decision making the body becomes a window to our thoughts (Damasio, 1999:51).

The body is ordinarily a window to our emotions, especially primary emotions such as happiness, sadness, fear, anger, surprise, or disgust. These emotions are complicated collections of chemical and neural responses that assist us to survive.

Background emotions such as well-being or malaise, calm or tension, are also observable. They are of interest because they can be triggered by external stimuli. They can also be produced by continued mental conflict, overt or covert, as they lead to the pursuit or inhibition of drives or motivation. We can perceive that someone is "tense" or "edgy," "discouraged" or "enthusiastic," "down" or "cheerful" by detecting "subtle details of body posture, speed and contour of movements, minimal changes in the amount of and speed of eye movements, and in the degree of contraction of facial muscles" (Damasio, 1999:52). Much of our internal experience is revealed on our faces, in our posture, and in our movements.

Subliminal influence is influence outside of the awareness of the subject. It uses universal action-reaction sequences called fixed action patterns to affect the behavior of a listener-perceiver. It is admittedly a form of manipulation since the practitioner is acting upon someone without the person's knowledge. Mediators, teacher and other professionals who rely on manipulation to accomplish their work differentiate between good and bad manipulation in terms of intention or purpose. Manipulation for the benefit of the manipulator at the expense of the subject is bad. Manipulation for the benefit of others is good. From a mediator's perspective, exercising subliminal influence reduces the level of unnecessary conflict and stress involved in reaching an agreement and increases people's commitment to solutions.

Specific nonverbal behaviors provoke specific responses in specific ways in response to specific nonverbal behaviors. These behaviors and responses seem to be universal. Human communications always involve three factors: content, emotion, and process. "Process" is primarily manifested as nonverbal behavior. Most people engaging in persuasion focus on content or what to say, but everyone knows that most of the message in communication is nonverbal which means that the bulk of the message is in the process. Process involves gaze and voice behavior, voice, posture, gesture, proxemics, and breathing. "Emotion" is also expressed nonverbally and involves the feelings component of interactions. Feelings are typically expressed as changes in pitch, skin color, pupil size, perspiration, and changes in muscle tone. Content, process and emotion are interrelated. For example, an attempt to send a message (content) using an inappropriate *process* (e.g., being too loud, too terse, or too talkative) or behaving in such a way that evokes an intense *emotion* generally interferes with the reception of content.

Effective persuaders design and deliver their messages to take the audience from where they are to where they want them to be. They understand that they have to take their audience on a journey. A good message is not enough; delivery is critical. A top-notch delivery requires the ability to manage nonverbal behavior for its effect on an audience.

Delivery is the difference between good and the best; and top-notch delivery requires the ability to manage your nonverbal behavior for effect, it involves reading the effects of your message and delivery on your audience and making real time adjustments.

The design of an effective process generally addresses questions like the following:

- ❑ How do I make a powerful and unforgettable point?
- ❑ How do I build rapport and get others to share resources with me?
- ❑ How do I project power and credibility?
- ❑ How do I demonstrate similarity or enthusiasm appropriately?
- ❑ How do I establish trustworthiness?

Key #1

Stop, look, listen (and feel) . . . Interpret later.

The most important skill in learning to read nonverbal behavior can be summarized in the refrain of an old song by The Stylistics "stop, look, listen to your heart." The title only partially covers the principle. The song advises us to "listen to your heart," but to be effective we must listen with our eyes, ears and hearts (or for people who do not acknowledge the use of their hearts – the gut). In any case, we need to feel, as well as use our eyes and ears.

People's nonverbal behavior is always sending messages. Your ability to read it depends on your ability to detect behavioral changes associated with people's eyes, ears, voice, and bodies. In order to fully understand the "message" being conveyed by another person, we must first understand the effects of the environment (physical and psycho-social) on the person and have some knowledge of the person's normal behavior under similar circumstances. It is their change from "normal" that potentially provides us the most information.

Environmental influences are important because they may induce specific behaviors that can be misinterpreted as a reflection of a person's attitude or thinking. For example, if a group's culture requires that a person of lower social status not look directly into the eyes of a person of higher status, it would be foolish to assume that the person is being "shifty" because they are avoiding eye contact. Cultures (ethnic, organizational and professional) have social rules that affect people's behaviors, especially in ritualistic interactions like negotiations.

Not knowing someone's idiosyncratic behaviors can also be problematic. One of my friends, Tom, likes to cross his arms during meetings. He finds this position to be comfortable, yet he has been made self-conscious by books on body language that suggest that people with crossed arms being defensive or close-minded. In order to reasonably attach meaning to someone's nonverbal behavior requires some understanding of that person's normal behavior. The question we must ask ourselves is, "what are they doing at this moment that differs from what they normally do?" If they have been crossing their arms all afternoon and they suddenly uncross their arms when you announce your proposal, the change might be significant. You, however, should be more interested in the change in skin color and muscle tension that preceded the uncrossing of their arms. People can control their arms, but they can't control their skin color; that's a different matter entirely.

Tip #1:   The body provides cues about people's information processing preferences.

The fact that my MBA classmate spoke very fast – so fast that he would slur his words at times, that he used very few gestures, and that he liked to make eye contact as he spoke "told" me that he was probably a visual thinker. His visual tendencies made the presentation of a picture of the situation even more important than it would normally be.

A variety of nonverbal cues are observable. Table 1 features the four sets of nonverbal cues (eyes, voice, body, and breathing) of interest in this book and descriptions of different positions and movements associated with each of them. These are the general cues to look for as you observe another person.

The process of reading nonverbal behavior starts with developing a baseline. It is important to establish a person's normal pattern of behavior. The answers to some basic questions should be sought. For example: Does the person make steady eye contact when they talk with you? When trying to answer a challenging question, do they break eye contact and what do they do? Is the person's voice normally flat or does it rise as he completes sentences? Is his body erect or hunched over when he talks or relaxes? Does he use his hands to talk and are his gestures big or small? It is important to note the answers to these questions and note the types of cues observed such as those described in Table 1. Part of the important being gathered at this stage has to do with when certain behaviors occur relative to the interaction. Noting how he spoke, gestured, and moved while he was relaxed versus under a little strain is valuable.

Once you have a baseline, you can start to collect data focusing on observed deviations from his normal nonverbal cues and when they occur. The timing of the changes is important because, for example, there is a big difference between a change in pitch when describing an interest in reaching an agreement and a change when introducing a new topic. The timing of each change is probably significant. Additionally, the nature of the change should be noted. There is, of course, a significant difference between a rise in pitch and a decline in pitch.

The greatest temptation in reading nonverbal behavior is to try to assign meaning to nonverbal behaviors too quickly. There are a few reasons why you should resist this temptation. First, you are likely to distort the meaning of an action by ising your own behavior as a reference point for understanding his behavior. You are likely to determine the meaning by asking yourself what it would mean if you did it. Whatever answer you arrive at will reveal more about you than him. Second, your concern is with patterns of behavior in context. Individual data points are not very meaningful. They become increasingly valuable as they start to form a pattern. In other words, a line on a graph that passes close to three or four points is far less meaningful than a line that passes through ten. The third, major reason for not trying to interpret cues too soon is that you will miss subsequent cues as you try to interpret earlier ones.

It is more important that you just identify cues and that you refrain from interpreting them until you are familiar with the individual. Postponing interpretation is important because it is almost impossible to see a "tell" or the subtle signs of receptivity to an offer while actively doing something else, especially talking or evaluating. Every time you start to assess a behavior you remove yourself from the interaction and lose track of continuing action.

It is important not to evaluate the actions of others prematurely. A premature evaluation is an evaluation before you have enough data, or making an assessment at a time that negatively affects your planned strategy. Making evaluations about what you like and don't like too early can lead you to send nonverbal cues that interfere with your objectives. Remember you are not the only person perceiving nonverbals; others are also reacting to your behavior. There are two obvious ways to avoid evaluating data too early. First, strategically identify opportunities for assessment and evaluation. These may be scheduled breaks or times when you will be able to excuse yourself. The better you know the process in which you are involved, the better you can plan to take "time outs" to make assessments. Second, learn to make simple notes of observations and circumstances so that you can do assessments later. Developing an idiosyncratic coding strategy is worthwhile. I am commonly asked to interview job candidates and I have developed a set of notations that can be written quickly and make little sense to others, but jog my memory about observed cues and the context in which they occurred. I review these at the end of the interview and attach meaning to the cues based on the candidate's whole interview performance.

"Tells" are recurring behaviors and therefore require enough careful observation to identify them and the conditions that evoke them. Since "tells" are often idiosyncratic they are only understandable if you can associate the observed behavior with a situation or emotional state. A "tell" is only a valuable if you can relate it to a situational condition or emotion.

A substantial aspect of the strategic use of nonverbal behavior has to do with watching for signs of receptivity to proposals or new information. People who are breathing abdominally tend to be receptive to what is about to be said or currently being said. This type of breathing indicates relaxation and is a sign that the listener-perceiver is open to perceptual stimuli and capable of thinking clearly. If they are breathing abdominally as you deliver your proposal and they continue to breathe that way, it is likely that your proposal was acceptable. Undesirable proposals tend to stimulate stress responses and people start to breathe shallowly and more rapidly, or even temporarily stop breathing altogether.

The phrase "stop, look, listen" is applicable to watching for "tells" and receptivity. Stopping refers to pausing so that information can be recorded or processed. A pause (a break in action) is necessary because of the sheer volume of the information produced during social interactions. It provides us with the opportunity to observe the other person's behavior without distraction. Appearing to be thinking about a proposal, examining your options, or appearing to be trying to generate new options are all ways to create a pause. Nonverbal behavior can also be used to create a less conspicuous pause that accomplishes the same objective.

Effectiveness in reading cues requires the ability to direct your attention appropriately and to appreciate the context in which actions occur. Being able to focus attention on a narrow range of cues makes it possible to deal with a manageable amount of information. The pause keeps you from missing important cues while talking or planning your next move as action is taking place.

Since important aspects of nonverbal behavior are idiosyncratic, it is important to pay attention to the "vocabulary" of the person in front of you. While some behaviors are understood to universally convey the same messages, the number of these behaviors is actually quite small. Fortunately, people are creatures of habit and the duration and emotional intensity of the negotiation process gives us enough time to see their habits. The key to success is to find patterns in their behaviors and to take advantage of them. Taking advantage of a habit isn't necessarily bad for them; it could mean helping them identify and satisfy real needs. The critical question to answer is: what do you see and hear them doing, and when do they do it? Always figure out what their normal state looks like (baseline) and then with an understanding of the situation, look for deviations from the baseline. Highly skilled observers see and hear a few significant nonverbal behaviors in the midst of a sea of nonverbal behaviors.

Tip #2:   Accurately interpreting nonverbal behavior requires recognizing a behavioral change and the context in which it occurs.

Negotiation is a ritualistic activity; and all rituals are predictable. Successful negotiations go through expected stages of activity leading to an agreement. Use this to your advantage to identify times to collect and analyze data. For example, people rarely dive into negotiations without some small talk. This stage of the process presents an excellent opportunity to get an idea of the person's baseline behavior. Most people feel free to be themselves while talking about their trip to the meeting, where they live, or the weather. You aren't concerned with what they say as much as what they emphasize and how they say things. Once you have this information, you can compare the person's baseline behavior to the behavior you see when they are making a proposal or responding to one.

Creating a meaningful shorthand to record behaviors and circumstances is critical to discovering patterns of behavior. It is important to have enough data to see a pattern, so you can discern "tells." With experience, you will start to recognize cues quickly and easily, and patterns will become apparent. Make sure that you record what you see and hear, and not your impression. It would be a mistake to record that he was "nervous" because it isn't descriptive of what you actually saw. It's an evaluation and you make that later in the process. Instead of recording that he was nervous, your notes should record the eye, voice and body characteristics that lead you to conclude that he is nervous. Once you interpret the behavior and note other behaviors that confirm that it is a sign of his nervousness, you can feel assured that whenever you observe that cue he is actually nervous.

Table 1. Nonverbal Cues.

Head	Position (inclined, centered)	Movement—forward and back
Hands	Position Supine, Pronate	Movement—forward and back,
Eyes	Position (location, defocused)	
Whole body	Posture; Location	Movement--shift, rhythmic
Breathing	Location (upper, center, lower)	Slow, medium, fast; shallow, deep; rhythmic, irregular
Word choices	Reflect Visual, Auditory, or Kinesthetic	

The Act of Observing

Effectively observing others requires relaxation and attention. This is easier said than done in a poker game or a high stakes negotiation. Regardless of the stakes, it is important to relax because your sensory acuity depends on it. Tense people don't see, hear, or feel well. You want to have relaxed and alert body. Being alert and mentally sharp affords you the ability to see openings and respond to them quickly.

Relaxation and mental alertness is the goal of anyone who wants to be influential nonverbally. A relaxed person expends mental and physical energy constructively, conserving it when it does not contribute to the solution of the problem and spending it freely when it does. Tension costs you flexibility and timing, two attributes that are critical to good negotiators, salespeople, and politicians.

Learning to be observant requires both pattern recognition and the ability to vary perceptual speed. Pattern recognition is fast and efficient, but it is not necessarily accurate or precise. Most people recognize things, but haven't really "seen" them. An art professor made this distinction clear to his audience in Chautauqua, New York when he challenged his listeners to draw the front side of their homes. Most people could not draw their houses; they could, of course recognize them, but they could only recall fragments of details. Under threat, pattern recognition is very valuable because it allows you to respond quickly.

Developing the ability to effectively observe nonverbal behavior requires sensory acuity and that requires practice. You must relax and avoid focusing attention on any particular part of the person being observed. Relaxation is a physical state controlled by your breathing and strongly influenced by your mental state. You will find that focusing on breathing and seeing will tend to relax you because it will distract you from thoughts about actions and consequences. Your attention must be diffused over a wide area so you can see the whole person, track stimuli and responses, and respond to openings quickly. Peripheral vision is also very important for observing nonverbal behavior. Most people rely on central vision to view another negotiator. Central vision is problematic because it works by focusing your eyes and attention on a fixed point. In peripheral vision, the eyes are focused on one point, but attention is expanded to a larger field. It is important to be able to expand attention over the area surrounding the object of attention by making full use of peripheral vision. Being too close to someone reduces your ability to use your field of vision, and hence your peripheral vision.

It is important not to neglect your sense of hearing. Studies indicate that auditory cues, when they occur close to a person, are responded to more quickly than visual cues. Attend to both visual and auditory cues, when possible. It is also important to note that focusing on gross body movements induce a faster reaction than focusing on hearing or seeing a specific cue. For example, you can react faster to someone shifting his or her weight than you can react to a change in facial expression (Lee, 1975).

Relaxation is a physical state influenced by our mental state. Emotional stress creates tension in the body. Elevated muscle tension is reflected in jerky, uncoordinated movements. Interestingly, tension is contagious. Jerky, uncoordinated movements tend to create stress in others. An observer does not want to accidentally create stress in the observed. When trying to establish a baseline, an observer wants to see the person in a relaxed state. The best way to accomplish that is to exhibit the coordinated, graceful movement that is a by-product of rhythmic and deep breathing.

It is important to use your eyes, ears, and body to observe. Be careful not to rely too much on your preferred modality (representational system) because doing so deprives you of valuable information. For example, a visual person will often position himself far enough away to see the whole person (head to toe), but this positioning involves a tradeoff. If the other person is primarily auditory and conveys a great deal of information through her voice, you may find yourself unable to detect significant subtleties in her vocal delivery. A female voice can be difficult to hear clearly from a distance where a visual person might comfortably process visual cues.

Balance is important in observation because it affects perspective and perception. Balance can only be achieved through correct body alignment. The feet, the legs, the trunk, and the head are all important in creating and maintaining a balanced position. It is easier to observe the person in front of you when you do not focus on any particular part of the person (head position) and you distribute your weight evenly across your derriere or feet. Too much muscle tension in the trunk is also an impediment to effective observation. Sensory acuity also increases when you are balanced, physically fit and well-rested.

Tip #3   Stop talking, soften your focus, and center yourself to increase perception.

Observing nonverbal behavior requires keenness of perception. The observer has to stay objective and focus attention externally; to actually see, hear and feel what is happening without attempting to evaluate it. Talking to yourself is evidence that you are not focusing attention externally. Talking to yourself impedes perception because it distracts you. Even worse is to start evaluating what you are currently experiencing. Not only do you stop experiencing what is happening anymore, but you are also unaware of the signals you are sending to the other person. Evaluation requires that you literally detach yourself from what is happening in order to go into your storehouse of experiences and compare them to what *was* going on when you mentally departed. Evaluation detracts from your ability to observe. Treat observation and evaluation as separate activities.

Diffuse Attention, then Focus

Every encounter with the environment and other people exposes us to a tremendous amount of stimuli or information. While you are looking this page of text, your peripheral vision is monitoring the area around you for movement, your eyes are taking in light and color, your ears are processing near and distant sounds, and you are experiencing the pressure of a chair or a floor and the temperature of the room. These stimuli are only part of the stimuli that you are receiving at any given moment. We have not even accounted for stimuli produced via interactions with others. Every channel, sight, hearing, touch, smell, and taste presents you with continuous information. Ray

Birdwhistell, a prominent communications professor at the University of Pennsylvania, estimates that as many as 10,000 units of information per second are being received by people they interact with their physical environment and others (Lewis, 1989). Given the enormous amounts of information being processed, it is important to not focus attention on any one set of stimuli. This requires us to practice diffuse attention as in when you watch a team sport competition. You take in the whole and periodically focus attention on an aspect of the action. The more adept you are at seeing the entirety of the interaction, the more effective you will be at reading nonverbal behavior.

There will be times when you will want to focus your attention just as you do when watching a basketball game. Critical moves, the entry of new players, and unexpected actions all tend to be good reasons to focus your attention onto a single person or an aspect of a person's presence. The easiest nonverbal cues to observe are eye movements, while the most difficult to discern and the most meaningful are breathing patterns.

Eyes. Eye movements are fairly simple to observe. The eyes are the "mouse" of the brain. Their movement indicates the part of the brain being accessed at any given moment. Movement up and to the left indicates the accessing of the non-dominant hemisphere of a right-handed person's brain. This eye movement often enables a person to visualize remembered imagery. A right-handed person moving their eyes up and in the other direction (the right) is typically accessing their dominant hemisphere to construct imagery. Right-handers trying to tell untruths can be expected to move their eyes up and to the right, then down and across to right.

Lateral (horizontal) movement to the right is indicative of an effort to construct language. In other words, thinking of things to say and how to say them. The person is literally moving his or her eyes toward their ears. When the eyes move toward the left ear or non-dominant hemisphere, the person is able to access remembered sounds and pre-recorded material.

Moving the eyes downward is a sign of "going inside of yourself" to experience feelings. Movement down and to the right is about accessing feelings either tactile or visceral. It behavior is commonly seen as a person recalls the emotions associated with an event.

A similar eye movement, moving the eyes down and to the left creates a very different effect. It facilitates internal dialog; it is observed when people are talking to themselves.

The eyes fixed straight-ahead but defocused, sometimes with dilated pupils make it possible to quickly access sensory information. The information being processed is typically visual, but not necessarily. This kind of vacant stare gives the person access to the representational system that he or she has the most skill at accessing.

Voice. Paralanguage is the vocal component of speech, yet it is separate from verbal content. "It includes pitch, resonance, articulation, tempo, volume, and rhythm" (McKay et al, 1983). Your attitude, mood, and the intensity of your emotions are all betrayed by your paralanguage.

Pitch. As your vocal cords tighten, the pitch of your voice rises. Pitch varies according to your feelings. Intense feelings of joy, fear, or anger cause your voice to rise. When the muscles of your vocal cords relax, as when you are tired, depressed, or calm, the pitch of your cord goes down.

Resonance. Resonance refers to the richness or thinness of your voice. The shape of your vocal cords, mouth, nasal and chest cavities determine resonance. Heavy vocal cords and a barrel chest tend to produce deep, rich voices. Conversely, thin voices seem to come from tight, thin vocal cords emanating from a thin body.

Articulation. Articulation refers to enunciation or clear pronunciation. Some people are so relaxed that the sounds in their words are slurred and the words seem to run together. Some other people speak very clearly, articulating every syllable clearly.

Tempo. The rate of speech conveys emotions and attitudes. An excited person speaks faster than a depressed person. Speaking very quickly can cause stress in listeners. Slow speech can be a sign of fatigue, boredom or indifference.

Regional cultures have a strong influence on tempo. New Yorkers and residents of most big cities speak much faster than people in rural areas. When New Yorkers interact with people from the rural southeastern United States, their lack of articulation and slow speed frustrates them. New Yorkers tend to think of slow speakers as dumb. Southerners tend to think of fast speakers as slick and untrustworthy.

Volume. Loud voices are associated with enthusiasm and confidence. Very loud voices, however, create stress in listeners. Their loudness is often interpreted as aggressiveness or an unfounded sense of importance.

A person of high status who raises her voice is informing a subordinate that they are in command and they should do what they are told. A soft voice suggests lower status and conveys the message "Don't attack me, I know my place, I know I'm helpless" (McKay et al, 1983:70).

A soft voice can also make someone feel safe. It is sometimes seen as a sign of trustworthiness, caring, and understanding. It can also indicate a lack of confidence, a feeling of inferiority, or a sense that the message is unimportant. Whispers can have many meanings and are best interpreted by the context in which they occur. A whisper or an extremely soft voice can accentuate communication. It can also convey intimacy indicating that "this is between us." Used in conjunction with a loud voice, it can be used to grab people's attention.

Rhythm. The cadence of a sentence changes it's meaning and can also relaxation. Rhythm determines which words in a sentence will be emphasized. McKay et al. (1983) uses the phrase "Am I happy" to make the point. If you vary the rhythm, you change the meaning. "Am *I* happy!" or "*Am* I happy?" Stress or the lack of relaxation seems to disturb rhythm by altering people's breathing. The resultant change in air supply for articulation coupled with the associated reduction in oxygen to the brain may be the cause of speech marked by hesitation.

The speed, pitch and tone of a person's voice indicate their mode of thinking at any given time. Visuals race through words trying to keep up with the pictures their brains are generating. Their speech is fast and they often raise their voice at the end of words. Visuals tend to have high-pitched, nasal voices that can sound strained.

Auditories enunciate; words are crisp and can be melodic. Sound is important to them and they use they voices as instruments. They are more likely than other people to vary inflection, tone, and volume. Their tone is clear and resonant and they tend to speak with an even, rhythmic tempo.

Kinesthetics (kinos) tend to mumble. They slur the end of words and pause every few words to breathe deeply. Kinos tend to exhibit a low, deep tonality. Their voices can also be breathy.

Digitals speak with a monotone voice. They tend to speak in the third person and are processing cerebrally without feeling.

Body. Visuals tend to be very erect. Their bodies are lean and tense. Since head position corresponds to eye position, it makes sense that the visual's is up.

The hand gestures of the visual are high and near the eyes. Remember that the military conditions people to process visually – who wants to wait until the enemy is close enough to touch them, will help you recall the visuals placement of hand gestures. Picture the stance of a soldier when at attention. This is a classic visual stance. The back is erect, the head is up, and the body is still; and the gesture associated with this position is the salute. The salute is a gesture made high and near the eyes in almost every military.

Auditories tend to position their heads as though they were on the telephone. They have a tendency to lean forward toward the source of the sound. Since they are processing sound, they do not need to use their eyes and will often not make eye contact with someone talking to them. In fact, some auditories will close their eyes to screen out distracting stimuli from their eyes. An executive I once coached, would actually close his eyes as people briefed him in meetings. Many people found this behavior disconcerting. They were not sure whether he was actually listening or if they should stop talking.

An auditory body tends to be neither full nor thin. It has a "medium build." It softens when the person is processing aural information and growing tense when the focus of attention is external. Auditory gestures occupy the space between the mid-chest and the mouth.

Whereas auditories lean forward, kinesthetics tend to lean back. They sometimes lean far back in a chair. These are the kids who fell of their chairs in classrooms. As adults they will often lean back and clasp their hands behind their heads.

There are two types of kinesthetic bodies. The first is full and soft and typifies the feeling kinesthetic person, while the active muscular body characterizes a person who is tactile and proprioceptive. In either case, the kinesthetic's posture is likely to feature rounded shoulders.

The kinesthetic's gestures are large and tend to reflect the level of emotional involvement the person has toward a subject. The more intense the feelings of the speaker, the larger his or her gross body movement. Many gestures are located around their midsection with palms turned upward.

Digital processors display a nearly motionless face and body. They move very little and their hand gestures are usually jerky.

Breathing. Breathing is an important indicator of feelings, attitudes and ways of thinking. Rapid breathing is often associated with excitement, fear, irritability, extreme joy, or anxiety. Anxiety or built-up tension tend to interrupt breathing and is manifested by short gasps for air. "Shallow breathing in the upper chest often indicates thinking that is cut off from feelings. Deep breathing into the stomach is more likely to be associated with feelings and action" (McKay et al, 1983:63). Interestingly, shallow breathing is a characteristic of visual processing; deep breathing is a characteristic of kinesthetic processing.

You can learn a lot about a person by watching someone's breathing while relaxed (to set a baseline) and while listening to a proposal or presentation of perspectives. Focusing on the rise and fall of a person's collar may be the easiest way to observe a person's pattern of breathing. Pay close attention to the rate and depth of the breathing.

The respiration of a person processing visually is fast. It is also high in the chest (thoracic). Visualization itself is characterized by shallow breathing.

An auditory processor breathes in the diaphragm or the whole chest. They rely on effective breathing to have the air necessary for using their voices as instruments.

A kinesthetic person's breathing pattern is slow and deep (from the stomach). The kinesthetic's breathing can involve a great deal of pauses as they search for words.

Key #2

Think Audience, Present Audience, Commit to a Feasible Goal

Take 'Em for a Ride

Two critical points are associated with this key. The first is that the audience determines the message; and the second is that the message marks a journey from a starting point to a goal. You have to figure out where the listener-perceiver is and take them forward from there. The path, the milestones, and the pace all depend on the audience. The better you know your audience, the more effectively you can guide them along the path.

The audience's values determine the path, while the markers, milestones and the pace are determined by its modality (sensory) preferences and decision making order. Only recently have we been able to specify the most appropriate markers and milestones based on the neuro-biology of the audience.

Think audience, speak audience, and commit to a feasible goal is sometimes called the 30 second formula. Thinking like the audience gives a speaker-sender a good idea of what to do to get someone's attention. Before you can persuade someone to do what you want you have to get his or her attention, hold it, and then orient it toward your idea. Lots of things can grab people's attention momentarily. However, holding it for more than a few seconds takes more effort. Since an individual's average attention span is estimated to be 30 seconds or less, it makes sense to provide a listener-perceiver a climax every 30 seconds.

Structuring a presentation to be a series of mini-climaxes leading to a goal is one of the best ways to maintain a firm grip on an audience's attention. The National Basketball Association seems to understand this idea and accomplished this by instituting a 24-second shot clock. The difference in the nature of the experience between watching a game of professional soccer and a professional basketball game seems to illustrate two points. The first is "keep it simple" and the second is that many climaxes make the game more exciting. The only obvious climax (emotional high) in soccer is when someone strikes the ball toward the goal, but it happens relatively infrequent. The action in the middle of the field can be elegant, but passing and defense is not nearly as stimulating as threatening to score. Pro basketball, on the other hand, is simple to understand and has a climax every 24 seconds.

Think basketball when you make presentations. Create mini-climaxes based on the characteristics of your audience. If you understand how they "see" things and what they think is important, you will have an idea of what will spark them emotionally. Treat them as though they are all kinesthetic. Give them a reward (a laugh or surprise) every 30 seconds or less. The real art is in being able to make that moment both entertain and move you toward your point.

Knowing the audience's thinking and communication style preferences gives you most of the information necessary to figure out how to get and hold their attention. The nature of the climax depends on their values, how they see you, how they see themselves, and how they perceive the situation they are facing.

When your objective is to encourage someone to make a specific decision that you favor, it is important to consider a concept called decision making order. It seems that everyone has a sequence of representational systems (for example, kinesthetic to auditory to visual) for making specific purchasing decisions.

Rapport is the Best Starting Point

Regardless of a person's modality preference (visual, auditory, or kinesthetic), they will see you as credible if they believe that you are sincere, open-minded, empathetic, and can make them feel safe. Before they'll even entertain most of these questions, they will make a decision about whether you and they are in rapport. If you have no rapport with them, you may not even get a real chance to be heard.

Assessments of rapport are often subconscious, unless prejudice is at work. Actually none of people's reactions based on prejudice really involve much thought. If you are visibly different than your audience, then you are likely to have difficulty establishing rapport from the onset. If the audience is not under stress, the fact that they are in the majority will provide enough of a sense of safety to allow a speaker to establish rapport. Regardless of whether you have a hostile or a friendly audience, you need to establish rapport quickly and introductions can do that for you.

The importance of introductions is determined by the culture of the group. In an elite setting, for example, in a room full of diplomats or high ranking officials of an institution, someone is expected to introduce you to the group. The level of esteem the group holds for that person and what he or she says about you is going to determine how much rapport you have with the group. It is important to make sure that what the person says about you reinforces your rapport with the audience – you already have some rapport if the group respects the person.

Your task after the introduction is to reinforce your rapport with the audience with your nonverbal behavior. Mirroring their behaviors, if they see you as a peer, is generally a safe strategy since elites tend to strongly adhere to their group's norms.

Elites generally operate according to visual rules in Western countries, so walking and sitting erectly, making small gestures, and speaking sparingly usually maintains rapport. Your next task is to establish your competence, trustworthiness, and dynamism as you interact. A good introduction cannot entirely answer all their questions, but it positions you to establish that you know what you are talking about and to start the process of giving them what they want.

Whereas the purpose of an introduction to an elite group is to establish credibility, in non-elite groups the purpose is primarily to establish that you are like them. A kinesthetic introduction will often be terse, but the degree of friendliness exhibited in the introduction will greatly affect the audience's response to you. The onus is then on you to establish your competence, trustworthiness, and dynamism by being charismatic and vigorous. A good introduction can help you establish the perception of competence, but your verbal and nonverbal skills complete their impression.

The orientation and thought processes of the audience determine the best way to structure the presentation of your ideas. The orientation of the listener can refer to their attitude toward the subject, the presence of stereotypes in their thinking, or a position they have staked out. As a good communicator you want to move a listener toward your position by taking the listener on a journey from where they are to where you want them to be. The better you show them that you understand where they are, the easier it will be to move them toward your goal.

"Speaking audience" is best accomplished by using the words and phrases that are common to them. The appropriate use of vernacular or specialized jargon facilitates establishing rapport and credibility. It is a nonverbal dimension of language that creates general comfort or unease in listeners. The operating assumption is that anyone who speaks like me understands my world and me.

The 30-second formula doesn't work for every audience. If you are truly "speaking audience," you will have to consider the social and professional characteristics of the audience. A three-minute formula may be appropriate for a kinesthetic audience. For example, an audience in rural Montana will generally give you more than 30 seconds for a variety of reasons. First, people in these communities generally talk slower. Second, they appreciate a good story and they tend to take their time telling one. And third, they tend to appreciate pregnant pauses that allow them to feel the emotions that surface during the story.

Establishing rapport with an audience is one way to "speak audience." This can be done nonverbally by matching and mirroring their behaviors. Techniques for establishing rapport have been described in books like *Influencing with Integrity* and *Instant Rapport* by Genie Laborde and Michael Brooks, respectively. Brooks (1989:21) states that, "being in rapport is the ability to enter someone else's model of the world and let them know that we truly understand their model. And it's letting someone come into our frame of the world and having an experience of them truly understanding us."

The general thinking about rapport is that when you match the other person's style of communication, you substantially increase your ability to influence their behavior. Put simply, if you talk like, sound like, and move like the person you are talking with, he or she is likely to be comfortable with you. It appears that the more comfortable they are with you, the more likely they are to talk candidly and be receptive to your ideas.

The components of matching and mirroring (doing exactly what you see and hear them doing) fall into the following four categories: eye behavior, voice qualities, body posture and gestures, and breathing patterns. Matching a person's voice tone or tempo is one of the most effective ways to establish rapport. Matching a person's breathing rhythm is another effective, although more difficult way to establish rapport. Being in synchrony with another person's breathing enables smooth conversation. Mirroring body posture and gestures is also effective, but more dangerous in that it can be detected if you are not subtle or lack timing. Paying attention to what your listener is doing with his or her body can help you determine how to interact with them most effectively from moment to moment.

"Speaking audience" is not as simple as it appears when it comes to persuasion. In order to effectively "speak audience" you have to understand how your audience prefers to receive and process information. Persuasion requires that you speak so that your message is heard, remembered and acted upon. "Speaking audience" in persuasive communication requires that we understand how the audience takes in and stores information.

The goal in "speaking audience" is to read a person's individual style (inputting and storage) and present your message accordingly. Their internal representation of sensory experience is for all intents and purposes the way they store information. People who see images in their head or mind's eye tend to store pictures of events and interactions. Those who experience feelings viscerally tend to become aware of feelings, while others whose experience involves sound may talk to themselves.

A person's culture greatly affects how they generally think, but it is most likely to have its most obvious effects on how a person expresses himself or herself (outputs). Don't be fooled into thinking that their expressive style is their preferred modality. How a person speaks *is* an indication of how that person thinks, but it may also be a reflection of the person's adaptation to cultural norms. The person's inputting and possibly storage is revealed when he or she is not talking.

You want to know how the person processes information so that you can deliver information to him or her in the manner that will have the most impact. People have the capacity to use all three modalities (visual, auditory and kinesthetic), but they prefer one. When a person is dealing with new, emotional, or difficult information, he or she temporarily loses the ability to use the other modalities and is forced to rely on his or her preferred mode of processing.

There are two major nonverbal challenges in "speaking audience." The first challenge is to secure the conscious or unconscious attention of the listener-perceiver. The most powerful influence is of course asserted below the level of awareness of the listener-perceiver. The second challenge is to enable the main points of a message to be fixed in the person's mind; and that involves the storage of information. Success is achieved when a message is delivered that has enough impact to be stored in the person's mind with an emotional charge. The emotional charge is not necessarily in the delivery of the message, but delivery greatly influences the storage and retrieval of information.

Securing attention initially is most effectively accomplished by appealing to people's lead representational system. People prefer to start from their lead system then shift into other modalities depending on the nature of the message and the task. The lead system is the portal, but the primary (preferred) modality is the main processing system. Whether you are making statements or asking questions, you will find that they understand more easily and can respond more effectively to statements and questions put in "language" of their preferred modality.

Visuals. People in a visual mode maintain eye contact with you and want you to maintain eye contact with them. If you do not give them constant eye contact, they will wonder if something is wrong. They talk quickly using pictures as reference points. Your pace should be fast and there is no need for a great deal of enunciation. In this state of mind, sound is not very important and precise articulation can actually be distracting.

People processing visually generally want enough room to see you. They prefer to be able to see you from head to toe. If you are not neat and punctual, you will find the interaction difficult from the start. Visuals will notice your attire and pay attention to the length of the conversation. They tend to be very conscious of time. They are more comfortable interacting with people who have an erect posture. They also value stillness; large hand gestures and too much head movement are distracting to them. Be fairly still, respect their time, and whatever you do, do not try to touch them unless they initiate the contact.

Talk with too many words will often cause a visual person to 'space out.' They appreciate words that allow them to make pictures, especially when the words allow them to either elaborate on their picture or 'change slides.' If you create a picture and then provide too much detail, they will doze off. For them, this experience is akin to showing them slides of your vacation one by one and droning on. They don't care about details like who you met, their names and where they came from, the menu at the resort, and so on. They want you to give them the overall impressions by showing them a lot of slides. A fast pace with pictures keep them engaged.

Many people in high-level positions are visual. This is one of the reasons why they are rewarded with offices with a view. They can see a great deal after being given a small amount of information. Since they are productivity-oriented, they are often busy people and appreciate fast-paced transactions. They speak in bursts and their voices rise at the end of phrases.

Auditories. People in an auditory mode tend to pay attention to your voice. You don't, however, have to possess a radio voice to hold their attention. If your voice connotes passion or enthusiasm, they will be enticed into listening to you. Leaning forward at the waist in their direction also draws their attention.

Rhythmic speech makes them comfortable; it builds a sense of rapport. Matching the speed, volume, and pitch of their voice creates quick and fairly deep rapport. Looking at him or her periodically also facilitates conversation. There is no need to make eye contact. They actually find continuous eye contact to be distracting. It can cause them to 'space out.'

The auditory will pay attention to the words you use. They tend to be literal in their interpretation of language. You can also count on them to know the secondary and tertiary meanings of words. They enjoy orderly presentations and will quickly point out a non sequitur because they distract and annoy them. Questions that do not follow a logical sequence and people who do not enunciate also annoy them.

It is foolish to interview an auditory person in a noisy environment. They will be distracted by the noise, especially if they can hear people talking. Loud places deny them the opportunity to talk to themselves and read between the lines.

A smart interviewer will allow himself plenty of time for an interview with an auditory. If they connect with you, they can "talk your ear off." Since there are few simple questions in their minds, it is important to be patient. Every question requires some background information and an orderly description of what happened. If they think of something they had forgotten to mention, it is not unusual for them to go all the way back to the beginning of a story so they can fit the information into its proper context. If they are particularly auditory, they will even replay conversations word-for-word, sometimes imitating the voices of the speakers.

Kinesthetics. In the kinesthetic mode, people tend to like to interact with someone who appears relaxed. The handshake is often the first indication of who you are to the kinesthetic. A weak handshake or a clammy hand can put you at a deficit from the start.

The kinesthetic likes to be close enough to touch you. In fact, they sometimes will touch you as they get interested in what you are saying, or as they try to get or hold the floor. Kinesthetic males like to stand along side of each other. That way they can be close enough to touch, but not have to endure eye contact. Many kinesthetic people do not like much eye contact; they find it distracting.

You also should leave plenty of time for interviewing kinesthetics. They may take some time to 'warm up to you' and they usually are not very talkative, so there may be a lot of silent periods. Additionally, they have to have time to translate feelings into words. If you make eye contact while they are trying to do the translation, they often have difficulty finding words. Interrupting them as they speak can also mean that you never get back to what they started to say. If a new feeling overtakes them, they go with it.

It is not usually difficult to know when you have excited a kinesthetic. They convey their feelings with their bodies, so when they are excited their gestures and movements show it. They may move more, or make larger gestures, and they often get louder. You can avoid staring at a kinesthetic by looking downward and glancing up only when he or she does. Speak softly and pause frequently, so that they have time to process their feelings.

Digitals. People in the digital mode, tend to sit as though they have a stick stuck up their spines, they are very erect, and virtually motionless as they talk. If you want to connect with him or her, you will want to be erect, motionless, and phlegmatic.

Digital people tend not to make direct eye contact with people, they may sometimes look toward them, but they do not feel self-conscious about staring in another direction. It is important to maintain a tight and motionless face to maintain rapport. The objective of dealing with a digital person is to pull him or her out of this state of mind. Otherwise, you will find yourself talking to someone who interacts with you like a police officer. If you recall the Joe Friday character from the movie or TV show called Dragnet, you know what the digital sounds like "Just the facts, ma'am."

This type of interaction is about control. They want to control the facts that they share as well as the flow of the conversation. They are often working according to a procedure or formula that they merely fill in with situational variables. Theirs is a world of templates, graphs, and formulae. If they appear to be detached from their feelings – it's because they are – and their use logical words and their deadpan delivery confirm it.

Decision-making order. People generally shift through all representational systems when transitioning from paying attention to something, to having interest in it, and then deciding to take action in response to it. They habitually follow the same pattern for specific types of decisions. Top salespeople have discovered that guiding a person through the appropriate decision-specific appropriate sequence for a particular decision facilitates decision making in their favor.

Interestingly, we seem to use the same routines to make specific types of decisions. For example, whenever some people make a decision about whether to buy a vacuum cleaner, they first test various models for how they feel when run across a carpet, they then listen to the sound of the engine, look for color they like, and then finally they may read about their its technical features or cost before purchasing it. They do this every time they by a vacuum cleaner. Oftentimes, by the time a person using this pattern gets to the price, they have already bought emotionally bought it, unless they get "sticker shock." Surprisingly, most of us are unaware of our routines, but we tend to use it them consistently.

A presentation that follows someone's decision making order makes it easy for them to say "yes." It feels comfortable (another way of saying that it feels safe). A skillful presenter guides us through our decision making process by reading our satisfaction in each mode and then moving to the next mode until the whole routine is completed.

Being able to communicate appropriately in each mode greatly increases our persuasive power. Using a person's decision-making order reduces the amount of energy and time required for persuasion. It also increases our chances of securing and holding their attention, makes our appeal consistent with their interests, and creates a sense of desire that leads them to say "yes" to our proposal.

Your first and most important step in the guiding the decision-making process is to get their attention. It is relatively easy to capture their attention by appealing to their lead system. For example, talking about the color of a car hardly makes sense when someone is primarily concerned with the feel of the driver's seat. This does not mean that they have no interest in color, but if they are like my mother-in-law, they need to know that the car will be comfortable to drive before considering anything else. For her the driver's seat and pedal position is critical. If the driver's seat doesn't fit her, she's not interested, no matter what the color.

Culture gives us some idea of people's decision-making processes and evaluation criteria. If the person is a member of a technical culture like engineering, they will tend to rely heavily on analysis (their digital mode) for decisions related to their field. Engineers will often examine the specifications sheets and prices of mechanical equipment (for example a vehicle or appliance) before they consider looking at it. They may then want to talk about the 'specs' with a technically knowledgeable salesperson or casually with a colleague, and only after feeling satisfied that their questions have been addressed will they then actually look at the object and make a decision.

It might surprise people to know that many techie audiophiles do not even have to listen to amplifiers before buying them. It is not unusual for us (yes, I have allegiance to this clan) to buy equipment from catalogues. A typical buying pattern for members of this group might look like the following. They might read the spec sheets, consider the numbers and the reputation the company has for quality control, then look at pictures of the equipment, and consider which records or CDs they intend to listen to as they consider amplifier, monitors, cartridges and other paraphernalia. Photographs of the equipment ensure that the design and color of the equipment doesn't clash with the rest of the audio-visual system. The most tactile of our clan may need to actually manipulate the controls for "their feel." A "sticky" or "tight" attenuator can be a deal killer for these people, but for many other audiophiles, the deal can be made without listening to the equipment at the shop. Besides, any former salesman knows the sound on the sales floor can be manipulated to make equipment sound better. They also know spec sheets from reputable manufacturers don't lie.

Our preferred representational sensory system modality (visual, auditory, or kinesthetic) greatly influences the type of input that captivates us. People who favor visual processes will often pay attention to things that appeal to their eyes. A small group of people uses their mind's eye to make images and need input that favors the construction of clean mental images. Those people who rely on their ears are likely to pay attention to the quality of a sound or voice. If the sound is melodic, it will often be appealing. My father, who was a musically inclined engineer, seemed to revel in the sound a well-made vehicle. This meant that he smiled just about every time he closed the door of his 1956 Mercedes. That sound signified quality for him. For my friend, the late Dave Phillips, the sound of a well-tuned engine could make him smile. Even when he was in high school, he could detect engine problems by listening to them. It should be no surprise that he also liked to dance. I helped him with fractions and he taught me to dance.

It Don't Mean a Thing If It Don't Stick

If you want a listener-perceiver to easily recall your message, you need to make it easy to process and store in his or her mind. It is likely that the person does not use the same strategy for processing and storing information from the environment that he or she used to obtain that information. In other words, he may pay attention to pictures, sound, or feelings in the environment, but primarily process and store sensory information (think) in another mode. People may think in pictures (in the "mind's eye), with internal dialogue (talking to themselves), or as emotional, visceral responses or physical reactions (Eicher, 1993).

Strictly thinking in terms of storage, some people naturally re-present reality to themselves as pictures, some use their mind like a tape recorder and re-present it as sounds, and still others store it as feelings. The most challenging communication involves translating information from one modality to another (for example, visual to kinesthetic or auditory to visual).

An effective communicator will use visual aids, stories, and props to make her points. In this way, she will create a sensory-rich tableau that appeals to everyone. Stories can appeal to every sensory modality depending on how they are constructed and conveyed. When told well, stories can create vivid images and intense feelings when told well. Gerry Spence trains attorneys to paint "word-pictures." to accommodate the average person's need for assistance in creating vivid mental images. Painting "word-pictures" is a form of strategic storytelling that designed to creates images that compel action. Word pictures are facilitated by a speaker's use of tone, volume, inflection, and pacing, and even space. For example, a fast paced delivery enables many people to form mental images, while slowing down enables them to experience feelings. Timing and pace are also important in the introduction of illustrations and props. Well-timed and choreographed presentations increase the likelihood of people storing critical images and feelings related to important points in a message. Spence often presents stories and graphics in a way that establishes a frame around an issue that enables a juror to discount or diminish the significance of contrary information.

"Speaking audience" is about offering the person information in a way compatible to their storage of information. This necessarily involves the form and style of delivery.

For example, when we speak to a visual listener at a fast pace and show her slides, she finds it easy to understand and remember the information. Such a presentation saves them the listener the time and energy of having to translate or repackage the message for storage.

Visual processors tend to think in pictures, diagrams and figures. Graphs and charts are easily stored in their memories especially if they illustrate or reinforce the logic of an argument. They are often concerned about answers to "why" questions. These answers address the underlying logic of an argument. Once they agree with the logic of a situation, they can easily retrieve information that supports or illustrates it.

Vivid images are the easiest for visual processors to remember. Color, clarity, size, contrast, and resolution enhance memory. The advertising industry is very aware of these variables and design ads to exploit them. Trial consulting firms also have large graphics departments because of the power of visual imagery and the importance of being able to translate important information into powerful visual images. Computer graphics specialists and photographers often assist attorneys in simulating accidents, depicting relationships between parties or complex data, as well as the impacts of crimes. They understand that a colorful image is easier to remember than a black and white image; that larger images have more impact than smaller ones, and that high-resolution images are more memorable than grainy images.

Visual imagery depicting movement is particularly powerful. The movie, *The Matrix*, illustrates the memorability of this sort of presentation. There are probably very few people who have seen the movie who do not remember Keanu Reeves arching his back in slow motion as bullets trailed by ripples of turbulence fly around him. Images like this one and other movies like the Wizard of Oz, Field of Dreams, Back to the Future, and Titanic often become part of our visual vocabulary. Scenes from movies and video images that become part of our visual vocabulary can trigger predictable emotional responses and associations, or even establish "facts" in people's minds as in the Abraham Zapruder film of the Kennedy assassination or the Rodney King beating.

Auditory processors typically appreciate the formulation of information in steps more than visuals and kinesthetics. The information is most easily stored if it follows a predictable structure and addresses issues in a practical way. They value consistency and order and can be driven to distraction by a logical jump or something out of sequence. They are predisposed to find flaws in arguments and can become fixated about a perceived non sequitur.

Auditories are gifted with the ability to do rote memorization. That does not mean that they totally understand what they memorize, but then again they don't always want to understand why something works the way it does. Their interest is in how to make things work. They have a natural curiosity about procedure and methodology without necessarily caring about the reasons or theories that underlie them. This is, in fact, one of the aspects of their nature that separates them from visuals. Tell them how to do it and they will follow the procedure religiously without any particular concern for the outcome because they operate from the assumption that the right procedure necessarily leads to the right outcome. They retain step-by-step explanations of things extraordinarily well.

They record information for storage, so the quality of the signal has a great deal to do with the quality of the storage. A bad transmission leads to a poor quality recording and the quick degradation of information. Auditory memories always have fairly short half-lives. It is very difficult to remember what was said word-for-word for a very long time. Just as the quality of a magnetic tape-recording declines over time, so does the soundtrack that the auditory uses to recall events. Rhythms and melodies, can however, increase the retention time of information. One of my friends discovered the power of rhythm and melody when he decided to make a rap out of key concepts for a science class after overhearing the basketball player he was tutoring recite all the lines to a 10 minute rap tune. The student got a B on the exam and was surprised at how easy it was to recall the information during the test.

The Johnny Cochran statement "If it don't fit, you must acquit" was very powerful and its effect stands as evidence of the power of the auditory memory. It is hard to know whether the comment was specifically designed to target the auditory or the kinesthetic members of the jury but it certainly resonated with both of them. It resonated with the kinesthetics because it was an elegant use of a prop – something they like. They remembered seeing (and on some level, feeling) O.J. Simpson theatrically trying to fit his hand in the bloody glove presented to him in court. And Johnny Cochran's simple, rhythmic incantation "If it don't fit, you must acquit," certainly resonated with the auditories. Auditories have a fantastic memory for rhymes. One powerful little phrase locked an image and logic into the minds of the jurors.

Simpson's courtroom display was particularly effective for making a strong impression on kinesthetics. Tactile kinesthetics remember physical actions and what adult has not experienced trying to squeeze into a glove that doesn't fit. Cochran knew that people would be disinclined to believe that someone would wear a glove that didn't fit to commit a crime. He also intuitively counted on the fact that kinesthetics are very prone to direct cause-and-effect thinking. They employ the "logic of gears" – everything has to fit together and move together in correspondence to work. A break in the logic chain is difficult for them to overlook. In this way they resemble an auditory person except kinesthetic chains are more tangible. A break in the chain of custody in handling DNA may have much greater significance to someone who likes tangible connections. Similarly, an argument about potential degradation by exposure to sunlight makes strong sense to the common sense mind of the kinesthetic. It appeals to their analogous thinking process. They know what happens when blood and other biological materials sit in the sun.

Props are very important for affecting kinesthetics. The bloody glove display was an excellent prop because it vicariously allowed jurors to experience the act of trying to fit their hand into a glove that was too small. The likelihood of the jurors having a vicarious experience was made even greater by the fact that some of the jurors identified strongly with the defendant.

Props are very valuable when presenting information to kinesthetics. They allow you to engage them by letting them touch something, even if vicariously. If they can actually manipulate an object or participate in a simulation, the shrewd communicator will have added another memory-enhancing dimension to the presentation – muscle memory. Tactile kinesthetics are prone to remember the physical sensation of an activity and relive it. This is one of the reasons why hands-on simulations are so effective. Muscle memory has the longest half-life of any form of memory. You never forget how to do things that have been learned kinesthetically like swimming, riding a bike, or tying shoelaces.

The prospects for securing attention and improving recall in kinesthetics are greatly enhanced if they are entertained. Movement, novelty and surprise draw their attention and create long lasting impressions on them. O.J. Simpson's theatrical display accentuating the difficulty of trying to place his hand in the bloody glove greatly increased the memorability of the moment for many kinesthetics, not because it was particularly entertaining but because it was novel and dynamic. It was also a major departure from the wordy, dry, tedious presentations they had endured for days.

Presenting Stress

The concept of "presenting audience" is also important in interviewing. Intentionally mismatching representational systems can increase the amount of information obtained in a negotiation or interview by temporarily increasing the level of stress in an interaction.

Sometimes inducing stress is a valuable tactic. It often can prompt someone to reveal what he or she was trying to conceal, or get him or her to elaborate on something that they sought to skim over. The choice of stressor should match the lead system of the person. For example rapid-fire questions may increase stress in kinesthetics and auditories, but have little effect on visuals. Conversely, what induces stress in a visual person may have little effect on an auditory or kinesthetic person.

Almost everyone responds to territorial incursions. That is to say, that encroaching on a person will generally create stress in them. Everyone has a distance where they feel most comfortable talking. These distances are culturally programmed according to many anthropologists, but they also correspond well to visual, auditory and kinesthetic processing. Visuals want the most distance between themselves and others in conversation, while auditory and kinesthetic people like the least. Encroaching on a listener-perceiver's space can greatly increase their levels of stress.

The effectiveness of other stressors is closely related to people's preferred sensory modality. In general, abruptly changing the way we do things in an interaction will cause stress in a listener-perceiver. This could mean stepping into him with eye contact, suddenly raising our voices, or changing the pace of our speech. Eye contact while encroaching on someone's space is very confrontational and bound to elicit a stress response in almost anyone, although a greater reaction can be expected in kinesthetics and visuals. Suddenly shouting will also cause stress in almost everyone, but raising your voice and talking loudly to an auditory, or for that matter, lowering your voice to barely a whisper and saying "important" things in the presence of an auditory person can cause a great deal of stress. The effect of the latter is to reduce the quality of the information they obtain in your message. Even your question is a source of information to an auditory person.

There are many ways to create stress in a questioning situation. Visual people tend to become stressed if you stare at them as they answer. They also tend to experience stress when someone abruptly changes the logic of a line of questioning. They don't like "being thrown curves." They are acutely aware of the trajectory of a conversation.

Visuals can also become disconcerted by tedious, highly articulated questions or questions with elaborate prefaces. Such strategies may interfere with their ability to create or maintain images as they answer questions.

Auditories will often react to abrupt changes in volume or tone. Not all changes of volume or tone are disconcerting, just those that are incongruent. They use words and sounds to make sense of reality. When words and pitch or volume do not match, their minds can become fixated on efforts to make sense of the discord.

Auditories often will feel much more stress if prevented from immediately responding to questions or sarcasm. When forced to be quiet and listen to something they disagree with, they can become very upset. Being cut off as they try to correct a misimpression or elaborate also creates stress and annoyance in them.

Since kinesthetics are generally not talkers, situations where they are forced to be sedentary and exclusively express themselves through language are often inherently stressful. Too much "seat time" is a stressor for kinesthetics.

Kinesthetics also don't like being asked questions in rapid succession, or being interrupted as they respond. Rapid questioning makes it hard for them to find words and causes confusion. Being interrupted has similar effects. They lose track of what they were going to say and become agitated.

Kinesthetics also tend to dislike eye contact, particularly when they are being questioned. This "turns up the heat" on them, and typically will produce an intense reaction although it is often not particularly revealing.

Telling Signs of Thought and Talk

Deciding how to craft and deliver a message depends on knowing and understanding people's representational systems. Representational systems tell you about how people think, what they focus on, and the values they use to evaluate situations.

There are a variety of external characteristics associated with preferred representational systems (modalities) or modes of communication. These outward expressions of modalities also correspond to the way people learn new information. The average visual person (shorthand for a person who thinks in pictures) is typically organized, neat and orderly. Their offices and bedrooms are tidy. They turn in assignments on time and pay careful attention to how things look. One manager I met annoyed his technical staff by insisting that every report submitted to him have "plenty of white space." His digital/auditory staff was convinced that he didn't pay attention to the contents of reports, but that he wanted them to be "pretty." An executive I once worked for demonstrated her visual tendencies by selectively reading the headings and bulletized items in my reports. Visuals like bullets. They are devotees of the 80/20 rule; they want 80 percent of the information in the first 5 minutes of a briefing and once they've created pictures in their minds want to be able to ask you questions to fill in gaps in the picture.

Visuals tend to move to the top of organizational hierarchies because of their ability to process a great deal of information quickly, respect to order, and their task-orientation. Westerners have a bias toward visual people. We think that they are smarter than other people, and we admire their ability to appear reserved and composed under stress.

One of the reasons why we think that visuals are smarter than people who prefer other modalities has to do with the fact that they do well on tests. Tests demand the ability to recall facts out of order – something the visual mind does with ease (Grinder, 1999). Most academic tests are constructed in such a way that people have to be able to mentally retrieve and rearrange information to answer the questions. This is something that a visual mind does naturally. An instructor of Distributive Education (part of the Distributive Education Clubs of America) in my junior year of high school trained our class to improve our memories by visualizing the physical filing of information into folders. Someone with a photographic memory (an extremely visual person) actually sorts through the material in her mental folders and reads the page that has the answer on it. One of my highly visual friends used his photographic memory to great advantage to get very high scores in a pre-vet curriculum. He got high scores in most subjects, but he could not "ace" physics. He could see the formula, but he could not use it effectively, unless it pertained to ballistics. Ballistics was easy for him because he could *visualize* the trajectory of an object in his mind, and he had an intuitive feel for the actions the formulas described since was a hunter.

Visuals also tend to be quieter than auditories (shorthand for people who re-present reality using sound and words) and kinos (shorthand for people who re-present reality using touch and feelings). They also tend to deliberate more than people relying on other modalities and they prefer to read, rather than listening to a lecture. They are quick to take your handouts and read them before you have a chance to present the material; and if in a position of power, are likely to derail your presentation by asking you premature yet penetrating questions – sometimes amazingly on point.

Auditories are not known for being particularly well organized or neat, but they are known for talking to themselves. They are easily distracted by noise and conversation and tend to like to socialize. They are the friends who can mimic dialogue and accents and who when asked to recall what someone said can repeat it word for word, often with perfect intonation and inflection. They live in a world of sound and often will spend a lot of money on high fidelity audio equipment. The movie "High Fidelity" very accurately depicted this particular subculture of the population. The main character compulsively made lists, rank ordered things, and had intense conversations with himself about important issues. Many auditories have large compact disc or record collections (often preferred) and the capacity to recall a specific "cut" on an LP and give you excruciating detail about when and where it was recorded, and by whom.

A couple of years ago, I gave a short survey to a group of clients to illustrate their thinking style differences. A visual person pointed out that the survey referred to record collections (visuals make great editors) and that I should update the survey to reflect the dominance of CDs. I thanked the person and later told him that I had considered changing the phrasing and elected not to figuring that people would know what was being asked of them, but more importantly because "real" auditories would probably still have record collections – I do. Many audiophiles actually prefer records to compact discs and many of my former stereo salesperson colleagues still prize tube amplifiers over transistor equipment. There is an audible difference between compact discs and records; compact discs are sometimes criticized for being "too bright." I must confess that I do not have the ability to discriminate between tubes and transistors, but some of my friends truly believe that they can.

Auditories learn by listening. They are people who tape lectures and go to discussions where authors talk about their work. They tend to like poetry readings, comedy shows, and concerts. Words and sound are translated into emotions and memories. And they tend to have exceptional memories, especially for steps and procedural sequences.

Many lawyers, project managers, old computer programmers and musicians are auditories.

Auditories can be distracting at meetings. First, there is no such thing as a rhetorical question to an auditory. If you ask a question, expect an answer in the form of a structured, linear narrative often with much more detail and background information than you wanted. Another distracting behavior is their tendency to "talk to think." Visuals really dislike this tendency because they think, then talk. They see doing otherwise as a demonstration of a lack of preparation, discipline or composure. Auditories don't agree, they are sharing their thought processes with you and inviting you to participate when they think out loud. There is an underlying assumption that the best ideas come from dialogue – well okay – argument.

Auditories pay attention to the sound quality of people's voices. They evaluate presentations and people according to the resonance or uniqueness of their voices. They are likely to comment about Demi Moore's attractiveness in terms of her voice. It's not that they are blind; they just process the world through sound and love mellifluous or unique, but pleasant voices. They can be driven to distraction by a high pitched or whiny voice. It is not unusual for them not to like the sound of their own voice when they hear it on tape.

Auditories remember what is said. They often repeat what they hear to themselves to make sense of, and "record," the information. If the person speaking has a unique voice, the message can be recorded and replayed for years to come. They have voice-activated memories and will often ask teachers what "something says" on a test even though they can read it. They unconsciously want to hear the teacher say the critical words to activate their memories. They talk to themselves or replay their recording of the teacher's lectures while taking the test. One of their biggest problems in taking tests is the inability to finish them. Since their minds work like tape recorders they have difficulty finding the information without "listening" to long tracks of the material they have studied. This process is quite a bit less efficient than the using the laser beam of the visual to find and play information on their compact discs.

People who prefer the kinesthetic representation system respond to physical stimulus. They like to touch people and stand close to them. They pay attention to room temperature, the feel of a chair, or the distance between a speaker and themselves. Kinos (shorthand for people who re-present reality through feelings and touch) tend to move more and use bigger gestures than auditories and visuals. When they are "moved" (something that connects with them emotionally), they move. Kinos have large physical reactions when moved by anger or passion.

Intense feelings and thinking do not go together. When asked a question, kinos will typically rely on their intuition and instincts (feelings) to respond; oftentimes having to move to think. Similarly, they memorize by seeing and doing or being "walked through" a process.

My Answers Tell You About Me

People answer questions in ways that reflect how they think. The structure of people's answers reveals their priorities, and even their motivation. Valuable information can be obtained from the way they order issues, their wording and omissions, and the energy used to express thoughts or feelings.

Kinesthetics. Kinesthetics like to tell stories to illustrate major points. The kinesthetic when answering a question of interest to him reveals his excitement in his face. His face becomes animated and his eyes light up. The size of his hand gestures seems to be proportionate to his level of excitement.

Do not expect well-organized answers. They tend to endorse a philosophy that folk singer Utah Phillips articulated with the comment "it's not up to them to make the point; it's up to you to get it." Kinesthetics tend to ramble. Their information is coded in feelings, and feelings are difficult to access and translate under stress. Expect long pauses between sentences as people work to translate feelings into words.

When kinesthetics do not want to answer a question or are afraid to disclose information, they will often work to distract or confuse you.

Efforts to put feelings into words often require them to look down or away from you to think. The latter creates the opportunity for them to become distracted by activities around them. An interview conducted outside as you walk side-by-side can often be very rewarding. Kinesthetics tend to find it easier to access feelings while they are engaged in some form of physical activity.

Visuals. Visuals enjoy organized presentations and will often anticipate your questions. Their foresight leads them to often think that they know where you are going. In fact, this tendency can get in the way of questioning because they are very likely to give you tactical answers to shape the interview or move it away from uncomfortable topics. They are also the most likely interviewees to object to a whole category of questions. These are the people who are most likely to have created the concept of face and will do a great deal to preserve their image.

Visual people can be very difficult to interview. If they are trying to avoid answering questions for whatever reason, they have a tendency to start blaming people or things for problems; some blame themselves, some blame others.

Visual people will often provide you with lots of facts to illustrate points. They do not display a great deal of emotion, and tend not to talk much about emotions. On those occasions when they do discuss emotions, they do so in a detached manner. They are much more comfortable talking about facts and being critical and judgmental of actions and people.

Auditories. Auditories love eloquence. They love eloquence in others, and they love it in themselves. Some auditories have been accused of liking to hear the sound of their own voices. A wise interviewer gives auditories plenty of time to talk. They construct elaborate narratives with clear beginnings, middles, and endings. They speak in complete sentences and paragraphs. They love details and will give you names, facts and figures. In discussing events, they will recall actions in chronological order and in excruciating detail. You need not worry about an auditory giving you who, what, when, where, and how information.

One of the reasons why auditories need a lot of time to talk is because they tend to go off on tangents. As they start to give you the context and fill in specific facts, they will tend to elaborate on facts and digress. When they are afraid to disclose information, they will tend to become super-logical. Ums and pre-constructed phrases such as idiomatic expressions are used as fillers or buy time as they sort through information and construct sentences and paragraphs.

Tip #4:   Values are wired into in our physiology.

Many years ago, a mentor, told me that he "could tell people's values" by looking at them. This seemed improbable since values are traditionally associated with socialization, but he was able to demonstrate a correlation between specific sets of physical traits and a specific set of values. For example, he proved that he was able to make associations between values and voice patterns. A flat voice pattern characterized by a drop at the end of a phrase shows a preference for task-oriented behavior (productivity). A voice that rises at the end of a phrase is correlated with an orientation toward relationships (Grinder, 1999). This simple scheme reflects differences in preferences for pace and priority, two of the major differences between cultures.

Productivity-oriented people speak quickly, often running words together to try to keep up with their thoughts. They also have a tendency to raise their voices at the end of each phrase. Relationship-oriented people tend to speak with inflection. Their voices rise and fall as they speak.

Having an idea of people's values gives you some insight about what the focus of a question should be to elicit a response, and how to ask it. People who favor productivity like direct questions, and they like to talk about pursuing or achieving a goal. They do not want to waste time. While they like direct questions, they also like to be in control and will attempt anticipate your questions

A relationship-oriented person will find questions about people and feelings to be interesting. They liked a relaxed pace and value the amount of time spent in conversation. You will need to allow much more time with someone who values relationships than someone who is task-oriented. Relationship-oriented people take longer to express ideas, and they expect to have enough time to establish a relationship before disclosing information the kind of information they think is valuable. Lists of facts do not appeal to them and they dislike questions focused on data.

Talking Audience Improves Data Yields

Sometimes it is necessary to do research to learn about how people think. This involves asking questions. While the answers obtained from effective questioning may not be directly applicable to the process of influencing others nonverbally, they are critical in persuasion. Two aspects of questioning are of particular interest to negotiators, interviewers, and mediators – how we ask questions and how listeners respond to questions. The main objective in questioning someone is to obtain as much information as possible in an interaction. Interestingly, most people ignore huge amounts of information by only focusing on the verbal content of the interaction. Everyone who has been taught active listening knows that communication occurs on two levels – what we think and what we feel. In spite of this, most people focus on we think. Our nonverbal behavior betrays what we feel.

There is a great deal of information about possible motivation, interest, and intensity in the emotional level of a message. "One rule of thumb used in communication is that 90% or more of an emotional message is nonverbal" (Goleman,

1995:97). Attending to nonverbal behavior gives you access to the emotional content of a message and increases both the amount and richness of information obtained in a communication. The following three aspects of questioning are of particular interest: 1) the construction of questions; 2) the delivery of questions; and 3) the way the respondent organizes and communicates an answer. In general, designing and asking questions that match the lead system of the listener-perceiver produce the best results. The most complete and comprehensive interviews involve moving the person through their range of representational systems, for example, from visual to auditory to kinesthetic to obtain the most possible information or gain the most influence in the interaction.

Preferences for how questions should be constructed and asked are associated with a person's lead representational system whether visual, auditory or kinesthetic. There are preferences for how questions should be constructed and asked associated with each representational system. Violating someone's needs or expectations can elevate their stress levels or even cause them to have difficulty answering questions.

Visuals tend to like questioners to talk at a faster pace than auditories or kinesthetics. Fast speech helps them pay attention and facilitates their ability to sort through and create mental images. Talking to them too slowly creates stress, as they have to expend additional energy to maintain their attention. Slow speech tires them out quickly and can cause them to withdraw (mentally or physically) from an interaction.

Visual people like questions that allow them to work with their mental images. They like direct questions and will often give brief concise answers to them. They are not particularly concerned with enunciation, and can actually be distracted by highly enunciated speech since it tends to be slower and stalls their picture making.

Visuals are the most likely of communicators to try to jump ahead of your questions. When being interrogated they measure their responses as they envision the traps that you are laying for them. Even when they are engaged in non-hostile interactions, they are likely to answer the question that they think you should be asking or try to force you to take jumps in your line of questioning because they can "see" where you are going.

Auditory people appreciate a well-crafted question and will sometimes compliment you on the quality of the question. They tend not to rush people through interactions and will pay careful attention to your inflection, tone, and syntax. They are also likely to parse meanings, which may mean precisely defining a critical term in such a way as to avoid being forced to answer a question such as questioning the definition of "is" as was done by former president Bill Clinton. Similarly, they may answer exactly the question you asked, even when they know that it is not the question you meant to ask. In an adversarial situation, they can actually enjoy misleading you through the use of nuance.

The auditory person is frequently very talkative once the questioner hits upon the right theme. They, however, tend to provide a great deal of detail; and there speech is laden with complex clauses and qualifiers. They rarely answer a question without giving background information or explaining the circumstances that caused him or her to draw the conclusion they are offering.

Kinesthetic people do not like to be questioned. Actually, they don't like to talk. They may be willing to show you things, but they don't generally want to talk about them unless they have passion for the topic. For them, talking takes a great deal of energy as they are forced to convert feelings and actions into words. They can answer questions about what they saw or did fairly easily, but interpretations of what things mean or meant are much more difficult. It is often easy to get lost in their answers because their talk follows lines of associations that are often being made as they talk. They are often structuring their thoughts about an issue as they answer questions, thus giving a listener the impression that they are "making it up" as they talk. Be patient with the kinesthetic; they will often go off on tangents that seem unrelated to the issue, but yield important tidbits of information.

It is important to note that all of us can become kinesthetic under stress. Anyone who has felt stupid in a physician's office or a courtroom can attest to the validity of this statement. New, emotional, and unfamiliar activities can put anyone into a kinesthetic state. Our ability to communicate verbally declines considerably during these episodes – something that can be particularly disconcerting to anyone who is ordinarily an effective verbal communicator. Of course, becoming self-conscious in such situations only makes the problem worse. There is little to be gained by pressing someone experiencing this kind of distress for information.

On a fundamental level, the nonverbal aspects of questioning involve what you, and the listener-perceiver, do with our eyes, voice, body, and breathing. As in a polygraph test, the interviewer is trying to establish a baseline. You want to know what normal is for them. This can be problematic in an interrogation because the situation itself prevents them from being totally normal, but even in these circumstances it is possible to help people relax enough to set a functional baseline.

The first thing to consider is the situation. Is it an interrogation, and if so, what type? I once briefly worked with some Adult Protective Services (APS) professionals who were confronted by a very different challenge than a police interrogator or auditor. They were often conducting interviews in the home of the suspected offender and had to be granted entry in order to conduct the interview. Additionally, they could not afford to alienate the suspect during the interview because they needed to learn about possible abuse from them and the victim who was often under his or her control and in the dwelling. Another reason for wanting to avoid alienating the possible perpetrator was that agencies often had to rely on the perpetrator to fix the problem, since victims (often a father or mother) were rarely willing to leave the household.

This type of interrogation is far more delicate and complicated than a police interrogation, although both are challenging.

The APS interview requires much more control of nonverbal behavior on the part of the interviewer. She must be able to assert authority without aggression to gain entry, and then manage her responses to questions so as not to alarm a perpetrator. If she becomes alarmed to early, he can terminate the interview before enough information has been gathered to take action. The objective is to make him relaxed enough to reveal what is going on and what may be causing the misbehavior so that he can become part of the solution.

Don't Just "Speak Audience" – Present Audience

"Speaking audience" is not as effective as "presenting audience" because most of the message in a communication tends to be in the realm of nonverbal communication. Speaking audience is basically about verbal communication. It relies on the use of words and the voice in a presentation. Whereas, "presenting audience" includes the use of words and voice, but also nonverbal aspects of communication including image, gaze behavior, posture, gestures, and the use of space. "Presenting audience" is far more robust than "speaking audience."

"Speaking audience" is, however, very important. What we say and how we say it greatly affects the results of an interaction. The importance of words and sentence structure including jargon, syntax, and semantics varies depending on the audience and context, but it is rarely irrelevant. It is generally important to speak the way the audience speaks because it helps you gain entry into their club. The hidden assumption underlying the inclination to accept someone who talks like a member of the group is that he or she probably shares our worldview. Understanding the meanings of words and sentences often comes from a similar understanding of the situations in which they are produced. The use of the wrong terminology undermines efforts to establish rapport or common ground with an audience.

"Presenting audience" involves using nonverbal behavior to appeal to the audience and as a channel for sending messages. Nonverbal behavior can set the stage for an interaction; it can frame it; and it can predispose people to listen to you. And to many people's surprise it does not have to be consistent with verbal behavior. In fact, it can override or mask the content of a verbal message. The television detective, Columbo, used the impression he made nonverbally of being a disheveled and disorganized to disarm suspects. Additionally, he often asked some of his most penetrating and confrontational questions as he was leaving the room so he could give the impression that the question had just popped into his head once they started to let their guard down.

It is possible to think of the people who share preferences for specific sensory modalities as representing a cultural group. Without going into detail, the fact that members share common characteristics, perceive reality similarly, transmit norms across generations, and have similar preferences for recognizing and addressing problems imposed by their environmental challenges loosely qualifies them as members of a cultural groups. One of the most significant cultural differences between visual, auditory, and kinesthetic cultures is the way they decide who should or shouldn't be taken seriously. Each group uses different evaluation criteria for deciding whether they are willing to be persuaded or influenced by a speaker.

Many people make a fundamental error in not appreciating that an audience's assessment of a speaker (especially when compared to their expectations) can greatly affect the impact of the message he or she delivers. Different types of audiences have different beliefs about whether or not someone should be congenial or credible to be influential. Additionally, the characteristics you look for to determine whether someone is credible or congenial depends on your preferred sensory modality. The following describes preferences generally associated with traits of visually-oriented, auditorily-oriented, and kinesthetically-oriented people. Not all people with these orientations behave according to these generalizations, but enough do to make an argument that these statements reflect norms.

Visuals believe that people who have composure are generally credible. They equate stillness and graceful movement with credibility and intelligence. They are also more likely to "judge a book by its cover" than other people which means that they have often made an assessment before a person opens their mouth.

Visuals are typically not very concerned with the congeniality of a speaker trying in a to persuade them. They are primarily concerned with facts and data; whether or not they like the speaker and other related concerns are secondary at best. In fact, they often decide whether or not to pursue a relationship based on their assessment of a person's credibility. In their minds, competent people have earned their attention and interest.

Auditories primarily make their assessment of credibility based on what a person says and how they say it. Enunciation, pronunciation, vocabulary and grammar are important variables in their assessment. The quality of an argument may be neglected by an auditory if the speaker enunciates poorly, or uses words inappropriately, or uses poor grammar. This neglect is not a manifestation of elitism; it is basically the result of "noise" interfering with their ability to input and process the message. A weak voice, poor diction, or an accent that affects the rhythm of speech not only impedes their ability to understand the content of a message, but may also lead them to almost instantly conclude that a speaker is not credible.

Auditories value congeniality and are much more likely than visuals to engage in relationship building before assessing credibility. Relationship building need not be interactive for many auditory people. They can experience a sense of bonding while listening to a speaker. The effect can be the result of a theme that they find poignant, the feeling conveyed in the presentation, the crafting of the language, or even the nature of an accent.

The connection between a person's background and the assertions the person makes can be just as important as the delivery of the story. Auditory people often expect a speaker to establish his or her credibility in presenting their case. They are unlikely to divorce the speaker's background from the claims he or she is making. They like well-woven narratives and consider the speaker to be as much a part of the story as the facts that he or she is putting forward. For auditories it is not just a matter of facts, it is also a matter of experience; and someone who can convey relevant experience in an interesting way that reinforces his or her assertions is often seen as credible by auditory standards.

Kinesthetic people are not very concerned with credibility. The kinesthetic is much more concerned with rapport. The expression "I don't care how much you know until I know how much you care" summarizes their perspective. They are concerned about a variety of issues that inform them about how they feel about a speaker. They unconsciously may ask themselves as series of questions. "How similar are you to me?" Are you genuine? Do I like you? Are your experiences similar to mine? Are your perspectives similar to their mine? The answers to these questions often determine how much attention they are willing to give a speaker. If they like you or see you as authentic, you are likely to be perceived as credible. They do not have to like you to listen to you. They do, however, have to feel that you are authentic. They will listen if they see you as "real."

Kinesthetics generally perceive people as credible if they have charisma, are authentic, or are known and respected by people they respect. Credibility is not established through reciting facts, although they are not averse to them. Credibility is established by having what is perceived to be relevant life experience or a similar background to the listener. The use of relevant metaphors or anecdotes often establishes credibility quickly.

Your image is important to audiences. Each representational group, however, perceives and attaches meaning to different aspects of your image. Regardless of how they make their assessment, this assessment will affect what they will believe in your presentation and what they will allow you to talk about and say. Your image strongly affects your power, credibility, or approachability greatly determines the effectiveness of your presentation.

Even though it is difficult to define what gives the impression of power, people know it when they see it. People generally associate power with height, but short men who move well can also be perceived as powerful. Moving well is the product of good posture, balance, and fluid movement. When people stand upright with shoulders relaxed and arms at their sides they seem to project power. Powerful people generally move in a well-coordinated, fluid manner.

We subconsciously associate purposeful, fluid actions with the three D's – Determination, Dominance, and Directness; all of these taken together create an impression of assurance and honesty. We can create impressions about each of the Ds by managing our nonverbal behaviors.

People make judgments about credibility and approachability every day, but they don't all use the same rules. Visual people tend to be willing to be influenced by people they perceive as credible. They make assessments about credibility and willingness to interact with others on the basis of what they see. Their assessment of credibility affects whether or not they will pay attention to you. In the following case, credibility meant the capacity to spend money. A few years ago, I was in Nordstrom's department store with my mother in Bellevue, Washington. Bellevue is a very visual place. Even the name of the city reveals how visual it is. Bellevue literally means "good sight" in French. Anyway, mom was not getting attention from the salespeople and complained to me that a couple of people had come in after her and were being served as she waited for help. I looked at her and concluded their lack of attentiveness was based on the assumption that serving other patrons would be more lucrative. As a former retail salesperson, I knew that good salespeople are constantly evaluating prospects. The assessment is usually made visually and at a distance, since making eye contact with a customer imposes an obligation to serve them (a retail FAP). It was easy to see why a salesperson might see her as less of a prospect than others in the store at the time. Her clothes were somewhat frumpy and she seemed tentative about how to get their attention. Forty years of living in semi-rural America had affected the way she presented herself.

When my mother told me of her concern, I whispered to her to imagine that she was back in Paris and interested in making a purchase at one of the stores on the Champs Elysee she used to frequent. Much to my surprise and pleasure, a metamorphosis suddenly took place. She stood tall and exhibited a poise I had not seen in years. Her shoulders became square and set back, her chin rose, and her posture became erect. All of those years of prep school conditioning suddenly became evident in her posture and movement. She had literally been taught to walk with a book on her head in her youth, and it became apparent. Within less than a minute – it actually seemed like seconds, a Nordstrom salesperson was asking her if she could be of some assistance.

So what caused the change in the sales staff's behavior? My mother hadn't changed her clothes, applied makeup, or flashed a platinum American Express card. They responded to her nonverbal behavior; to the change in her demeanor. Salespeople routinely evaluate people's capacity to pay. Over time, they learn to associate certain patterns of behavior with buying potential. The most seasoned salespeople evaluate your composure, as well as your clothing. The salespeople who came to assist her were responding to their perception of her and a mental image they had of a good sales prospect.

Experienced Nordstrom salespeople know that clothes are not as good an indicator of social status (analogous to buying potential) as bearing, especially in areas where people have "old money." Some have learned hard lessons about judging people by their clothes. It may be a fairly accurate means of assessing the buying potential of yuppies and the nouveau riche, but they are not the best indicators for assessing "old money," and older people in general. Older people are generally less concerned about what people think of them than younger people, so they are not as apt to dress up when going to the store. And people from Mercer Island, Medina, and some of the nicer parts of the Seattle area do not always feel the need to "wear their money." Their casual clothes are not as good an indicator of who they are as how they carry themselves.

Auditory people make assessments about willingness to be influenced based on social acceptability. If people they respect "sing your praises" or vouch for you, they will listen to you. Their assessments are largely based on whether or not you fit into their notion of community. The following incident from my undergraduate days in college illustrates the potential importance of such assessments. A friend of mine, Sam who was a blue-eyed, light blond-haired sophomore had just entered a room full of Black male undergraduates watching an NBA playoff game on TV. He had been greeting people – many of whom he did not know, when a friend in the room started poking fun at him. Sam, without thinking, responded the way he normally did with his friend. It was the way almost everybody in the room would have responded to such a provocation. The only problem was that it involved the use of the "N-word." Within moments, he realized that most of the people did not know him and that he – a white guy, had just used the "N-word" in a room full of Black people. He froze as all the Black guys seemed to turn in unison, look at him, and then turn back to the television without saying anything. No one even made a face or gesture. This perplexed me. I asked my friend Marcus, an African-American from Oakland, California who understood Black inner-city culture to explain the group's reaction. I expected them to have attacked him verbally, if not physically. He was outnumbered eight-to-one. Marcus laughed and told me that the point "was not what he said, but how he said it." He explained that he had "said it like us," so we treated him like one of us. In retrospect, I believe that it was not only the way he said the word, but also his body language when he said it. Sam moved and talked like "a brother."

Kinesthetics don't seek credibility in speakers either. Their interest in relationships predisposes them to be more susceptible to influence by people who are charismatic or approachable.

Certain professions have high concentrations of kinesthetic or visual people. For example, designers tend to be visual and mechanics tend to be kinesthetic. Physicians tend to be visual and auditory. While there is some variation among physician specialties, the selection process for admission into medical schools seems heavily biased toward selecting visual/auditory people. This bias is largely due to the heavy reliance on test performance and GPA for qualifying for admission into medical schools. Getting good grades in college generally means being able to listen to lectures, write papers, and participate in discussions as well as recall detailed information quickly and effectively during tests. Students who can effectively input information visually and auditorily, are thus receiving instruction (and being tested) in ways that are most compatible with their learning processes. Additionally, the visual mind is very well-suited to respond to the demands of classroom testing. Its large capacity for storing information and rapid recall capability also gives it an advantage in taking timed tests.

Biases for visual/auditory people notwithstanding, there are kinesthetics among the physician ranks. They tend to be family practitioners, psychiatrists and pediatricians. The skills and aptitudes needed to be effective in these specialties tend to be associated with kinesthetic traits. Interestingly, the demeanor necessary to work well with children as a pediatrician is seemingly at odds with the demeanor required to get into medical school. A former roommate, Dan, experienced this conundrum. He applied for admission to medical school with what appeared to be excellent credentials. He had been a teaching assistant in a medical school curriculum, had a 3.8-plus grade point average in zoology, his father was a well-respected oral surgeon, and he had letters of recommendation from some prominent medical school faculty members. One day I asked the physiology professor for whom Dan worked what he thought of Dan's prospects given his background. I thought that Dan would be a top candidate since he was the kind of multi-dimensional candidate that med schools claimed they were seeking. After all, he was a scholar and an athlete (he was also a teaching assistant in physical education), a socially conscious person, and someone everyone liked. I also added that he wanted to be a pediatrician and that kids really liked him. Dr. Clark let me complete my list of Dan's merits, agreed with me, and then said, "He won't make it through the interview process. He doesn't have the demeanor of a doctor." I was perplexed. What did that mean? Years later, after spending time with physician and veterinarian classmates in epidemiology at the University of Washington School of Medicine, I understood what he meant. Physicians are expected to project credibility and confidence, even when they don't know the answer – which is more often than most patients would want to know. It turned out the characteristics that made Dan so appealing to little children probably set the interview panel against him. He was too easy-going, empathetic, and approachable. In short, he was too kinesthetic for them. After all, how many physicians would you describe using these terms?

Deciphering and Sending Messages

All people encode reality (memories) and their messages. Listeners (or receivers of messages) decode messages. The coding process is affected by our senses. Senses collect data: eyes collect pictures, ears collect sound, and the body collects feelings and sensations.

Your senses help us re-present reality to yourself. We perceive and code reality in terms of pictures, sounds, smells, tastes and other sensations. Each of us trusts one sense more than the others. These are merely tendencies, since all of us can and do use all of senses to interact with reality and code memories. Our preference affects our breathing our body posture and our eye movements.

When we meet people who share our representational systems or modalities, we feel comfortable. This is because "people like people like themselves." You can artificially create rapport by matching people's qualities of voice, posture, and gestures. People's choice of words can also create rapport but since we are concentrating on nonverbal behaviors, we will not cover this topic.

Information Processing

Visual Processing. Visual thinkers are the fastest information processors. They think with pictures and generally need to begin the learning process with an overview of the topic and a presentation of a purpose. Once they understand the big picture, they will pursue details. They tend to label information before noticing details. They are normally very cautious until they have a clear picture of the content and often the process to be used.

A visual thinker memorizes pictures. The most sophisticated of these processors have photographic memories. These people can literally see a page of text or a diagram and read it in their mind's eye.

They learn effectively from watching demonstrations. They like to observe, notice and watch, then imitate. Learning vicariously comes naturally to these people.

Visual thinkers are fond of creating systems based on the aggregation of the parts, details, and specifics that they have focused on. Their natural inclination is to look for the structural aspects of the situation.

Visuals have foresight with vivid imagery. They see details and possibilities. They are future-oriented, are natural planners and have the tools for effective long term planning. They organize thoughts by writing them down and tend to extrapolate from current patterns into the future.

In recent years, people have discovered the significance of visual information processing in the right hemisphere of the brain. This type of visual processing is very different than left hemisphere (traditional) visual processing. Right hemisphere visual processing is not mediated by words; it is entirely image or sensation-oriented. Dr. Temple Grandin, the famous autistic animal scientist, describes her thinking in the following way, "during my *thinking* process I have no words in my head at all, just pictures" (Grandin and Johnson, 2005:17). Grinder (1994) refers to this type of visual person as a "right-brained visual," while Kreger Silverman (2002) calls them visual-spatial learners (VSLs).

Visual processing in the two hemispheres is procedurally and substantively different. Visualization in the right hemisphere involves concrete three-dimensional objects, whereas visualization in the left hemisphere involves abstractions of reality. The left hemisphere uses with symbols like words or numbers to represent reality. The difference can often be seen in mathematical preferences. Left hemisphere visuals tend to like algebra and right hemisphere visuals tend to favor geometry.

The right hemisphere "readily synthesizes, allowing the individual to see the whole, and the other [the left] analyzes, dissecting the whole into parts that can be compared, contrasted, and placed in hierarchical order" (Kreger Silverman, 2002:26). The left hemisphere processes information sequentially and cumulatively. Grinder (1991) describes the process as "parts to whole" to suggest that information is considered step-by-step leading to a logical conclusion. The right hemisphere, on the other hand, uses a totally different approach. It uses a "whole to part" strategy. People who think this way prefer to work from the big picture down to the details. In many cases, they either understand the point right away, or not at all. Since their information processing is nonverbal and marked by a "Eureka!" moment, they are often unable to explain the *thinking* that led to the conclusion.

Kreger Silverman (2002) states that studies of middle-schoolers suggest that a third of the school population are probably visual-spatial learners. They may be a minority in the classroom, but they are a majority in some professions like geology, architecture and art. Both of these professions demand visual-spatial skills and aptitudes including the ability to think spatially, visualize in three dimensions, imagine physical objects, and recognize underlying physical and conceptual patterns.

While visual-spatial learners are visual, Grinder (1991) suggests that they really are kinesthetic people with high visual ability. The following comments by Springer and Deutsch (1998:306-307 in Kreger Silverman, 2002:12) seem to support his perspective: "although they are characterized as more spatial than the left, it [visual-spatial thinking] is probably more accurately described as more manipulo-spatial, that is, possessing the ability to manipulate spatial patterns and relationships." The idea of manipulation is kinesthetic. My wife, Susan, and many other architects can create three-dimensional images in their minds and rotate them in the way that AutoCAD programs do. In fact Susan specializes in space management using the integration of kinesthetic and visual processing to walk through imaginary space and experience what the client will experience. She can look at a set of blueprints, create a mental "CAD design" and then experience where the sun will strike someone as they enter a room or whether the space will feel restrictive or expansive.

Although visual-spatial strategies are visual, they are often also very kinesthetic. Temple Grandin's advice to a client having problems with an animal is that he or she "try to see what the animal is seeing and experience what the animal is experiencing" (Grandin and Johnson, 2005). Grandin uses the integration of visual and kinesthetic sensory stimuli to design extraordinary facilities for animals. Right hemisphere visual processes seem to naturally synthesize visual and kinesthetic experience. The same idea can be seen in the practice of the Chinese art of Feng Shui. On a simple level it appears to be primarily a visual art involving the positioning of objects in rooms, yet high-level Feng Shui practitioners like my wife Susan and her master use their ability to *feel* energy to make design and spatial decisions.

Strengths of Visual Processing

Visual thinkers are generally labeled intelligent by North American society. Their speed of processing is highly prized and they are capable of thinking about many things at the same time. Multi-tasking is a natural skill for visuals.

A classic visual has the ability to focus internally. They are capable of great concentration.

They have a large capacity for information storage and can process that information very quickly. Their output is usually linear and conventional. While their work products are typically not very original, they are generally organized, detailed and accurate. Additionally, the work is likely to be submitted on time since they are very time conscious, enjoy planning and scheduling, and place a high value on punctuality.

Weaknesses of Visual Processing

People who are primarily visual processors have trouble remembering verbal directions and information. They "space out" or daydream if they are verbally overloaded. Disorderly, nonlinear information distracts them.

They are apprehensive about taking risks if unsure of their ability to complete the task perfectly. This tendency can lead to the three Ps: perfection leading to procrastination, leading to paralysis.

Auditory Processing. Auditory people cannot help but talk. They talk to themselves and they like to talk to others. Many of them think out loud. When considering new or difficult topics, they often explore them verbally. Emotionally difficult situations will often distract them for long periods as they ruminate about what they could have said and should have said while replaying dialogue repeatedly.

Auditory learners are attentive to sounds and learn by talking and listening. The quality of a voice can enhance their ability to remember information. It is not unusual for a highly auditory person to repeat what has been said out loud to improve his or her chances of remembering it. They will often start the sentence with "in other words . . ." and then put the content in their own voice. Many highly auditory people (auditories) have voice-activated memories. They remember what has been discussed.

They enjoy lectures and discussions. Talk is their means of learning and socializing.

They have difficulty processing information that is not clearly articulated and linear or sequential. Things that involve steps and procedures are easy for them to remember and understand. Numbering each step of a process also facilitates learning.

It is important to verbally entertain one option at a time. They have a tendency to get confused by a non-sequential presentation or having to track more than one scenario or option at the same time. If they are unable to talk, they also may find themselves unable to listen.

A discussion of the pros and cons of situations and proposals is important. Failure to do so will set up the likelihood of auditory people distracting themselves with internal dialogue about issues of interest to them. They talk through problems and try to arrive at solutions verbally. Understanding comes through the use of reasoning skills as they process information one-step at a time.

If you want to enhance the prospects of an auditory learning new information repeat it in short phrases. They need repetition for learning. It is also important to use tone, tempo, and volume systematically.

Strengths of Auditories

Auditories can follow complex steps and procedures. They also have good short-term memories. Most auditories learn very well in social situations such as group discussions and debates.

You can rely on auditories to be able to repeat (parrot) information back with great fidelity. The highest functioning auditories can recall large tracks of verbal information word-for-word, from speeches, conversations, and discussions. These auditories are also exceptionally good at rote memorization and recalling facts. One must, however, be patient after asking an auditory for factual information. They cannot help but provide context and detail in their responses that many listeners may find overwhelming or distracting, particularly if you are short of time.

Weaknesses of Auditories

Random sounds distract auditories. This tendency is predictable since sound is such an important part of their lives. Rhythmic, harmonious sound actually comforts auditories.

Auditories have difficulty remembering visual information and instruction. Interestingly, you should not be fooled into thinking that an auditory person who "parrots" back information really understands the concepts underlying the information. Since words are important to auditories, it should come as no surprise that they have good spoken vocabularies. They also remember and recognize names easily.

Punctuality can be a problem unless they develop a systematic approach to time management. Their interest in relationships and talk can lead them to "waste" time talking about what they are going to do or "war stories" at the expense of meeting deliverables.

Auditories often run out of time in test situations. Their decision making process is slowed down by the need to mentally replay lectures to find pertinent information as they answer questions. Finding important information can be like trying to find a favorite song on a cassette tape.

Kinesthetic Processing. Kinesthetic processors are the slowest processors of information. They remember an overall impression of what was experienced and store the feelings associated with the experience. Retrieving feelings and then putting those feelings into words takes time. A dominant kinesthetic bases their knowledge on impressions, hunches, intuition and feelings. They express enthusiasm when available choices match their values and personal interests.

Passion drives their behavior, and entertainment holds their attention. They exhibit random bursts of energy and interest.

Strengths of Kinesthetic Processing

Kinesthetics can block distractions to internal processing. Noise and voices do not easily distract them when they are internally processing their feelings.

Kinesthetics enjoy the act of discovery. There is great potential for entertainment in discovery, and they really like entertainment. They are usually willing to explore and create new choices if the exploration process allows them to simulate or field test choices.

Kinesthetics tend to have a global perspective. This may be related to the fact that they tend to operate using intuition and hunches, which means that they are unconsciously including many factors in their assessments of situations.

Kinesthetic memory lasts the longest. We never forget how to do things that we have learned kinesthetically like riding a bicycle, swimming, and skiing. Kinesthetics remember what has been done before.

Weaknesses of Kinesthetic Processing

Kinesthetics do not like to plan. They tend to live in the "here and now" and do not feel the need to plan, nor do they seem to have strong aptitude for it. Planning diminishes spontaneity, and kinesthetics like to preserve choices.

Kinesthetics have a tendency to "dive in." They are impulsive and sometimes illogical. They do not use logic for decision-making; they prefer to use instinct and intuition.

Kinesthetics appear to be inconsistent, in part, because their actions are motivated by feelings and they are so susceptible to emotional shifts. Additionally, they participate until they run out of energy. The quality of that work varies with their interest in a topic.

Kinesthetics (kinos) want to feel emotionally involved. Stimulating intense feelings improves the memorability of an experience. Adding touch can also enhance their memories. Trial and error approaches to learning make experiences more memorable for kinesthetics.

Give kinos the opportunity to manipulate objects to increase their learning. If they can actually perform the task, they will learn tasks more easily. Kinos enjoy "hands on" learning experiences. Craft trades such as plumbing, welding and pipe fitting, are dominated by people with high kinesthetic ability and many have institutionalized their preference for hands-on training in "on-the-job" training and long apprenticeships.

Kinos tend to need more frequent breaks than their colleagues in meeting situations. They get restless and distracted if they are not given the opportunity to move periodically. Kinos need to doodle or move their hands. This appears to be the behavior of a distracted person to non-kinesthetics but it actually helps them process information and keeps them on task longer. Once kinos are distracted, it is difficult to get them on task again without letting them release some their energy by doing an exercise or letting them have a break.

The physical environment can greatly affect the performance of tactile kinesthetics. Uncomfortable chairs, rooms that are too hot or too cold, or confined spaces shorten their attention spans and stimulate undesirable behavior.

Feeling kinesthetics are greatly affected by the emotional atmosphere of a setting. They have great difficulty accessing their own feelings when encountering the intense emotions of others. Feeling kinesthetics are inclined to be empathetic.

Effective storytelling that allows an audience to experience the actions and feelings of another person appeals strongly to all kinesthetics. An effective story "moves" them. They will actually move in the seats, shift their weight, or actually get up and walk around when you deeply affect them.

It is important to note that kinos look for patterns and tend to overlook details. They remember the most recent material presented to them best. Recent items leave the strongest impressions, unless impressions of earlier material were intensified by strong feelings.

The key to effectively facilitating their learning experiences is to establish and maintain a relationship with them. They respond to rapport, not rules. They prefer the opposite approach to visual processors in terms of the structure of learning experiences. They want to see the application of an idea before they show interest in the concept underlying it. Once enticed to pay attention to the concept, physical movement helps to reinforce it.

They prefer to look at materials as members of a group, not individually. When working with someone one-on-one, they prefer to be side-by-side. Kinos want to take action with the belief that they can make corrections en route to the answer. This belief compensates for their disinterest in planning.

Tip #5: Acknowledge issues and concerns before trying to discover needs.

Simply stating that you acknowledge people's issues and concerns is insufficient to get them to engage in self-disclosure. Your nonverbal behavior strongly influences whether they disclose information or engage in some form of self-protection. A harsh, loud, or shrill voice obviously does not encourage openness, but neither does a stiff body. People interacting with others who are loud or stiff will often protect themselves by becoming quiet, or they will become prone to lose track of what they are thinking and feeling as they are distracted by the tension of the situation. Passive people experiencing stress can actually be observed forming a protective ball like armadillos – the torso shrinks, arms are held close to the body, and they adopt a modified fetal position. Other people exhibit the opposite tendency in response to elevated levels of stress hormones; they become aggressive.

Tip #6:   People won't reveal their needs (the drivers of conflict) in an environment devoid of safety.

Trying to ignore resistance just gives people the opportunity to time their attack. By putting their resistance on paper you convert it to something symbolic. Setting the symbol aside nonverbally allows you to postpone the issue until it is fits into your presentation. If you don't put it on paper, you end up having an impromptu discussion in which you are trying to convince people to trust that you are not discounting their concerns. It is hard to convince someone to have faith that you will give their issues the time and attention they deserve. Most people won't let you do this gracefully until they trust you. Even if they do allow you to proceed, you have now lost your momentum or train of thought. There is also the possibility that you come across as being impatient or too forceful, thus threatening relationships. I recently watched a pair of presenters actually damage their relationship with their audience by not coordinating their response to resistance. One presenter was encountering resistance from the audience about his controversial opinion, when the other presenter who was sitting in the audience tried to offer a comment by asking, "Can I say something?" The other presenter, who had been very soft-spoken until then, suddenly responded with a sharp "no," then realizing the impact on the audience, softened a bit but still firmly said, "it is important that you don't interrupt because I want them to experience the tension of the situation." The audience suddenly started shifting in their seats and appeared to be uncomfortable. They actually empathized with the seated presenter who had just been "put in his place." The standing presenter could have spared himself some conflict if he had written the audience's objections on paper. The audience was having difficulty articulating their objections and this would have served to help clarify them. If nothing else, it would have forced the audience to work to make clear statements. The seated presenter later admitted that he was responding to his discomfort with the tension and was trying to relieve it. By not having negotiated with each other about how to deal with resistance before the presentation, the standing presenter was forced to treat his partner like a member of the audience (which is what he was in the mind of the audience) and abuse him. He could have avoided a big problem had he known tips #7 and #8. The first stating that: if you want to enforce boundaries (or rules) and preserve your relationship with participants, do so with as few words as possible. The more words you use, the more likely you are to come across too forcefully.

Tip #7:   Don't wait for resistance. Put it forward early, if possible, and then set it to the side.

There is nothing worse than a "what about" question when you have momentum or are just about to close a deal. Don't let people destroy your momentum by giving them good reason to interject their resistance or ask a distracting question. An additional benefit of putting objections and concerns in writing is that it provides you the opportunity to preserve the quality of relationships by managing misbehavior while drawing attention to the materials.

Tip #8:   Put people's concerns (reasons for resistance) on paper so you can deal with them when and how you want.

Putting people's concerns on paper helps you control your presentation process. When there is little trust between people or people feel unsafe, they either distract you or themselves during your presentation. Both safety and trust, in these circumstances, are associated with the suspicion that interests will be neglected. Some people will interrupt a presentation to ensure that their issues are addressed. Others will talk to themselves and disregard much of is going on around them in favor of their internal dialogue. It is possible to avoid either problem by letting people see that their concerns will be addressed. Note that once you have put people's concerns on paper in a *visible* place, you have an obligation to address them. If you fail to assure them that you will address their issues in a reasonable way, they will still be distracted or distract you.

Tip #9:   Don't locate the problem in the same space as the solution; separate the locations.

The expression "locations have memories" refers to the effect of physical space on our mental states. Almost everyone can think of a place that makes him or her feel good. Oftentimes, these are places where good things have happened to you. Similarly, there are also places that elicit bad feelings such as places where you have had violent fights, where you were humiliated, or where you experienced sadness for whatever reason. Just entering physical spaces associated with bad feelings can trigger memories, or actually initiate the process of reliving the experience. Most people don't think about the fact that this phenomenon affects negotiations too. For this reason, we should avoid trying solve problems in the same physical location where we experienced the pain and negativity of the problem. Think of the space associated with pain as "contaminated." Don't mix the good with the bad. Even a moderate change of location like moving to the other side of the room can prevent contamination of a problem solving process. Fortunately, if the problem is on an easel, just moving the easel moves the problem away from you. Put the problem on paper.

When They Feel It, You've Got 'Em

Persuasion works best when you know your audience well. Knowing whether their preferred modality is visual, auditory, or kinesthetic tells you a lot about their needs. Their wiring tells you what they are prone to pay attention to, how they will like things packaged, and their basic values. No matter what their preferred modality, they will ultimately have to derive pain relief or pleasure from your proposal or goal. If they don't feel it, they won't really commit.

Over a decade ago, I saw Tony Robbins deliver a seminar about persuasion in which he said that everything humans do is motivated by one of two reasons: a need to avoid pain or a desire to gain pleasure. He also explained that the main task in a sales transaction is to get the other person to clearly associate pleasure with your proposal or goal. Reading nonverbal behavior improves the prospects for accurately linking your proposal with their idea of pleasure (a desirable state). Once this is accomplished, all you have to do is deliver the proposal in a manner that appeals to them considering that only an estimated 7 percent of the message lies in your choice of words. Robbins' main message was that 38 percent of your message will be conveyed by the quality of your vocal presentation and that the remaining 55 percent (the majority) will be expressed through gestures and posture.

Tony Robbins (1990), who has made a successful career of using his persuasive power to sell his programs and audiovisual materials, presented a seven-step model of effective persuasion:

1. Turn yourself on.
2. Become their best friend.
3. Qualify them.
4. Give it to them.
5. Get them to commit.
6. Make it easy.
7. Create a compelling future.

The persuasion process starts from the moment that someone sees you. Every subsequent interaction affects your prospects for success. Before you ever meet them, you have to assess your image in their eyes and manage your nonverbal behavior to fit your strategy and their expectations. If you have diligently observed them and fine-tuned your presentation to their needs and expectations, by the time you are offer a proposal, they should be predisposed to accepting the offer.

1. Turn yourself on. The first step in persuasion begins with managing yourself. Passion, enthusiasm and credibility sells. Credibility can be established nonverbally by posture and countenance, the use of the voice, and reputation. Enthusiasm is, however, the projection of energy. People respond to your energy level, which may be the reason why Robin Williams and Billy Crystal are reputed to do sit-ups and calisthenics before they go on stage. Their preparation rituals indicate that they know that you can manage your state of mind by managing your body's physiology. Excitement breeds excitement and first impressions have an impact on how people respond to you, and ultimately, your proposals. A bad first impression complicates efforts at persuasion.

2. Become their best friend. Many skillful people mirror or match the nonverbal behavior of others to quickly gain rapport. These artificial strategies are unnecessary if you concentrate on making others feel comfortable and pay attention to how you and they breathe. If they are comfortable physically and psychologically because your presentation style fits their needs they will start to see you as a friend.

3. Qualify them. The objective of step two is to allow you to discover what they really want and how they'll know when they're getting it. Discovering their values requires detective work. People often don't consciously know their values; and if they do know their values, they rarely know how they would rank them. Fortunately, their bodies provide us this information whether they want to or not. People also tell you what's important to them by the choices they make. You can directly ask them what is most important to them and sometimes get good information, but you really learn people's values by finding out what they will and won't give up. Once you know what they want, you want to know how they know they're getting what they want – in other words, their evaluation criteria.

Understanding their values gives you an understanding of the standards that they use to make decisions. Reading nonverbal behavior to learn what they like and dislike will allow you to fashion and present effective proposals. Remember: the key to persuasion is to help them experience a desirable emotion when they encounter your proposal.

4. Give it to them. Step four is focused on having them experience your proposal. The actual strategy depends on how people process information, but the best persuaders create multi-sensory presentations. You want people to see, hear, feel, and even, smell or taste the proposal.

5. Get them to commit. Step five is about getting people to commit to your proposal. Getting them to state their commitment verbally starts the process of

securing full commitment. Getting them to commit to specific times for taking action moves us further toward overall commitment. Developing a sense of obligation by encouraging a sense of obligation or conscience almost cinches the deal.

6. Make it easy. Step six is about making the deal easy to make. Addressing problems or objections before others raise them helps make commitment easy. It facilitates the perception of safety thereby reducing people's self-doubt. If you identify objections before they do and you deal with them effectively, people are inclined to trust you. The two most predictable major objections are, of course, time and money.

Noting and handling objections by using visual materials has great impact. First, materials prepared before objections are encountered indicate that you are interested in, and know something about, an audience's needs. Additionally, visual materials made in response to their comments reassure people that their concerns will be addressed. Third, it facilitates the systematic and disciplined exploration of objections. If the nature of the objections you cite reveal a real understanding of their values, you also get credit for appearing to either know them well or be genuinely concerned about them.

A favorable side effect of managing their objections well is to make it easy for them to say yes by allowing them to relax and be in a favorable state of mind.

Paying attention to their breathing tells you when to present your proposal. If you have handled their objections and made them comfortable, their breathing will indicate receptivity. Packaging and presenting your proposal according to the way the individual prefers to make decisions also makes it easier for people to say yes.

Effective packaging and presentation of a proposal helps people to remember important facts and issues, thus making the deal easier to contemplate. Remember that commitment is typically a kinesthetic phenomenon. You commit with your heart, not your head. Help them experience the proposal and you will create long-term memory and ownership of the proposal.

Building a relationship with people helps cement commitment because it creates a sense of obligation and promotes the development of a conscience regarding the impacts of their actions. People hate to turn down a friend.

One way to reinforce commitment to the agreement is to find a symbolic means of representing an important associated idea or concept. A unique prop or physical symbol that represents the idea given near the peak of the emotional experience has lasting impact. Additionally, a significant change in your behavior and the context of your interaction with this person increases the salience of the event and the power of the prop. That's why people have closing ceremonies. An effective prop delivered during the high point of a ceremony can make all the difference in terms of ensuring the durability of the deal. An effective prop is distinctive enough to be an unmistakable reminder of the commitment, but isn't something that the person will hide or put in a closet (Grinder, 1989).

7.   Create a compelling future. The final step in the process is to create a compelling future – a visual and emotionally potent image that maintains desire and momentum. You want negotiators to see themselves doing what they say they will and living happily according to the terms of the agreement. The more vividly and specifically the picture of the future you can paint, the more compelling it is. Part of painting a compelling future might involve people seeing themselves and others interacting (for example, talking and working) in the new context.

Dealing with Resistance

Resistance can be viewed as a special case of incongruence since part of the person wants to do something and the other part doesn't. They want a change in their current condition, but they have mixed feelings about prospective changes. Resistance creates the platform for negotiations, and the behavior associated with it tells us something about what the negotiator values. Acknowledge resistance up front. It gives the resister less choices and it gives you more choices. Once you acknowledge resistance, the big choice is to fight it, or to flow with it. Labeling the resistance seems to relieve people of the obligation to continue actively resisting, and when acknowledged sincerely, it allows the resister to feel validated. Putting it on paper with the appropriate label converts resistance to a static object.

Acknowledging resistance can be used as a peremptory strike. If you acknowledge someone's resistance before they have a chance to make the point, you control how the resistance is presented if they can't object to your presentation. Your presentation presents a golden opportunity to circumvent hostility and vitriol.

Labeling the resistance and making it visible allows you to defer dealing with it. It also prevents unnecessary discussions about tangential issues that flow from the resistance process. You have the opportunity to cut off digressions indirectly by asking "how does that differ from what we've already recorded?"

There are different possible approaches to resistance. Labeling resistance and placing it on a board or flipchart paper is a visual approach to dealing with resistance. Once the resistance is acknowledged it is put off to the side. An auditory approach to resistance might start with a statement of the purpose of a proposal. Acknowledging resistance from one spot in a room and moving away from that spot to work on solutions is a kinesthetic way of dealing with resistance. Physically moving the symbol of resistance (record of issues or positions) out of the way has both a visual and a kinesthetic effect. The potential reasons for resistance can vary from legitimate specific concerns to prejudices and closed mindedness. Closed mindedness is, in fact, one the most common causes of resistance so we'll explore it. Four possible factors produce it.

1. Some people always see glasses as half empty. About 40% of the U.S. population is motivated by avoidance of pain or a fear of loss (Bodenhamer and Hall, 1997). They are people who are energized to avoid things more than move toward what they want. They have a tendency to be distracted by the past as they deal with the present by recalling all the problems they had when making decisions about products, services, or ideas. The motto of these people is "change is bad" (Lieberman, 2000).

2. The person has a visceral dislike of the presenter. The problem in this circumstance is not with the proposal; rather, it is with the messenger. "A visceral opponent is an emotional adversary, who not only disagrees with your point of view, but disagrees with you as a human being . . . Attacking 'face' is what causes someone to become an emotional enemy" (Cohen, 1980:189). "Face" is about public image or how you want others to think of you in terms of prestige, worth, dignity, and respect.

    Damage to "face" is a psychological or emotional experience often associated with the process of negotiations. The negotiation process gives people some indication of their social standing or how they are being perceived publicly. Procedural matters like seating arrangements, who gets materials first, and the order of issues on agenda can all cause damage to "face." Perhaps, more subtle and interesting are people's reactions to interpersonal dynamics. Negotiators have gotten upset because the other party consistently failed to make eye contact with them as they talked but did so with others, or the short pause between their statements and the mediator moving to the next agenda item appeared to suggest a lack of interest in their statement. Paying close attention to people's reactions to your actions can allow you to make mid-course corrections that prevent damage to a person's "face."

    If you make a visceral opponent of someone realize that they will not change their opinion of you quickly or easily. All the logic, facts, ideas and evidence you marshal will not be enough to persuade them. "If he hears it from you, he wants no part of it" (Lieberman, 2000:72).

    People who see other people as visceral opponents exhibit some telltale signs. In one mediation session, a highly visually-oriented woman refused to look at the other party. Her behavior was not unusual for a visual person dealing with someone who repulsed her. A person's preferred modalities affect the way they treat visceral opponents. Auditories tend to ignore the person and tend to try to communicate with an intermediary, whereas a kinesthetic person might just literally keep their distance from the person.

3. The person has not recovered from another unrelated situation in which he felt abused or manipulated, and the wounds are still fresh. Anything that differs from his usual thinking or preconceived notions is not going to be embraced. "He's not feeling good about his ability to make decisions and will retreat to safe ground to avoid being swayed" (Lieberman, 2000:72).

4. The person has a situational aversion. This means that the problem has nothing to do with you. Instead the whole concept or idea does not appeal to her on a fundamental level. "It's just not me" is what she is internally processing. In other words, your proposal is inconsistent with her self-concept (how she see herself).

Arguing with people like these will get you nowhere. "The stronger your argument becomes, the greater their rejection of it" (Lieberman, 2000:73). Persuasion in these situations is not about logic; it is about understanding them and giving them an opportunity to act according to their values and attitudes.

A stubborn person is one who is rooted to some belief or thought. They appear to be immovable; and they generally are if you apply direct pressure as in arguing logic or facts. Linear arguments based on facts are not as valuable as circular movements in these circumstances. The stubborn person has taken a position and is using the power that comes from their stance to push my proposal away. In order to resist they have to direct their energy against my proposal. They are essentially pushing on my proposal. Your task is to "lead" the opponent's power and mind. You do this by changing her focus and getting her to redirect his energy in a way that is favorable to your desired outcome.

For people whose objections are associated with the first three factors, you can apply a two-step process to facilitate a change of mind. First, you employ circular movement by changing his focus. Don't go head-to-head. Change her focus by making a statement about her values or beliefs that is consistent with your request. You want her to "agree to agree to an idea or way of thinking that will later neutralize her own objection" (Lieberman, 2000:73). Use your understanding of her public image, self-image, or core values to do this. If the person sees herself as open-minded, you can her to agree with the statement, "Don't you think that close-mindedness is such an unappealing trait?" "Then after a short time when you raise the issue find her unusually cooperative and open to your suggestions. Because once she "readily agrees with this statement she's unconsciously driven to act in a consistent manner" (Lieberman, 2000:73).

Sometimes you don't have to even make a statement. In the early 1980's, I found myself in the forest with a group of environmental protesters objecting to the use of herbicides to suppress weeds in a national forest near Flathead Lake. I was the regional manager of these programs at the time and had chosen to go out by myself with them to show this group the weed infestation and entertain any suggestions that they had to remedy the situation. The only constraints on their solutions were that it had to be performed within a month of our meeting and for no more than 25 percent of what herbicide treatment would cost. At some point, one of the young men became very upset and started yelling at me. He was literally "spitting mad" and was less than six inches from me as he initiated a tirade about the Forest Service and herbicides. I remember trying to listen to him and fighting the urge to move away or push him away. In a short time, his friends actually moved him for me. They had been articulating values about fairness, respect for life, and standing up for defenseless creatures. Seeing my willingness to treat them with respect, and then seeing their associate mistreat me seemed to violate their notion of who they were and how they felt people should be treated – even Forest Service employees. From then on, they listened to what I had to say without interruption as I had done with them, and we ultimately came to a mutually satisfactory agreement.

People have a need to behave in ways that are *congruous* with their attitudes, beliefs, and actions. All of us are aware of people who talk or think one way and behave in another way. We think of them as "flaky," "confused" or "hypothetical." We make the same judgments about ourselves. Once we commit publicly to a stance, our attitude will conform to it, and then influence subsequent actions.

The second step involves restricting her ability to do what she doesn't want to do. Yes, what she doesn't want to do. "When someone is stubborn it's because he knows that he *can* do something but *chooses* not to. By thwarting his ability to do it the equation is now thrown off because he no longer sees the decision as his. *And if you can't do something, then you have no reason to be stubborn about it.*" This second step works magically. While it is a verbal tactic, it can be greatly augmented by nonverbal behavior.

An acquaintance of mine, Tom, is very gifted at dealing with stubborn people using this two-step tactic. I can recall him trying to convince someone of the need to take action to correct a downturn in his performance. The person recognized the problem, but generated a host of excuses for why he couldn't take the action Tom recommended. Finally, Tom looked at him and said, "I guess you're right. You really can't get a contract with this new client. You don't have the ability. In fact, I am surprised you were even able to get out of bed to see *me* today." He then proceeded to give him a list of reasons why he couldn't get new clients. As he spoke, I could see the man pull back his shoulders, straighten up, and defiantly tell Tom to "F_ _ _ Off," followed by a list of things that he would do to get the client. As Tom turned away he said softly, "I was just saying what you said. I was agreeing with you."

What I had witnessed was the man's ego being activated and the creation of the unconscious desire to do what was being denied him. Once the desire to *be able* to get the new client is triggered, it's followed by the *desire* do it because of cognitive dissonance. We like to have our thoughts be consistent, so our thinking is, "I want to *be able* to get this client because I must *want* to get this client. The mind then begins to race for ways to do what it feels it must want to do" (Lieberman, 2000:74).

This tactic was made effective by Tom's control of his nonverbal behavior. He nonverbally restricted the man's movement by squarely standing in front of him, looking him in the eye, and assertively enumerating his limitations. As Tom noted the man's growing defiance, he prepared to assume a non-threatening posture. When the man aggressively objected, Tom quickly turned sideways in a simulated ducking maneuver as he softly told him that he was merely repeating his own comments. The man is now confronted by no real source of resistance. He has the power and the psychological incentive to take action.

Restrictions, especially time restrictions, work to get us to take action. That's why salespeople tell you that their offer "expires at midnight." If we can choose to take action at any time, our inclination to act is less strong. Manufacturers of Cross pens and Maxell audiotape may be taking advantage of this idea applied in the reverse. Both companies offer lifetime guarantees and rarely have to honor their offers. The key to an effective restriction is that it must be something that is overcome when *the person* creates a solution.

Lieberman (2000:75) lists six "power tips" for dealing with a person who becomes adamant. The first is a nonverbal behavior. 1. Change the person's physiology. If you can get a person to move, you can get him to change his mind. "When our *body* is in a fixed position, our *mind* can become similarly frozen." If they are standing get them to sit, if they are sitting get them to stand. You don't have to force the other person to move. You move and they will often move to adjust their line of sight. "Numerous studies overwhelmingly concur that there is no easier way to snap someone out of a mode of thinking that to *get him to move his body*" (Lieberman, 2000:75).

Tip #10: If you want people to shift positions or perspectives, get them to move physically.

2. Give someone additional information before you ask them to reconsider. The more you interact with someone the more information you get about them. Additional information can be an elaboration along the lines of an expressed interest, information that is consistent with the values or attitudes they have revealed, or a reminder of something he's forgotten. It does not have to be persuasive in and of itself because the purpose of providing new information is to allow him to make a *new* decision based on *additional* information instead of having to simply *change his mind*. Additionally, every new piece of information slightly modifies his stance by causing him to change perspective.

3. Increasing the person's self-awareness makes them easier to influence. This actually works in a literal and figurative sense. Lieberman (2000) talks about

research indicating that actually seeing yourself in a reflection increases the prospects of someone persuading you to change your mind. He recommends having a conversation by a mirrored wall or reflective panel.

This seems to also work on a figurative level. Skilled salespeople have recognized that people will soften their stance in the presence of family and friends who know them as amicable and pleasant. People generally don't like to see themselves as obstinate and aggressive in the eyes of someone close to them. The car salesman who invites your wife into the process may be taking advantage of this tendency.

4. Reciprocal persuasion describes people's tendency to change their attitudes about something in response to your request if they have previously gotten you to change your mind. Similarly, if you resist his request and you then ask him to change his mind, he will typically refuse to change his mind. Reciprocation works particularly well when you are able to link the change in your position to the new request. I can recall this working in a national forest after making a statement like the following concerning a proposed herbicide application. "After hearing your explanation of the need for a larger buffer zone, I think that I'll expand it from 100 feet to 200 feet – just to play it safe. Given that change would you be willing to support the plan."

The effect of your accommodation is heightened when you show that you had to think about it. People like to see that you had to reflect a little about the decision. A strategic pause while showing signs of deliberation always helps encourage reciprocity. A "hmmm" (for your auditories) with a break in eye contact and perhaps a stroking of the chin all contribute to reinforcing the impression that you had to think about the change. Don't expect reciprocity if they think that the change was not significant.

5. Studies have shown that presenting your side as well as theirs to a person holding an opposing view facilitates persuasion. Ignoring the stubborn person's opinions tends to make him think that you are discounting the validity of his perspective. Since there is usually some fact or truth in support of their position, it makes sense to acknowledge it and present both sides of the issue. Taking advantage of the impact of first impressions leads Lieberman (2000) to suggest that you present your side first. My inclination is to present his side first and do it well so that he is not countering my argument in his head as I talk. It is also consistent with the practice of aikido—a martial that relies on the redirection of force. In aikido, you move people in the direction of their force, take them a little farther, and then redirect them.

6. Let him think that he is, in some way responsible for the idea. This helps him identify more closely with the objective, thus allowing him to see his behavior as consistent with some aspect of his belief system.

These tactics work on three of the four factors involved in making a person stubborn. They do not work if the person has a situational aversion. In this case, the entrenched belief is connected to his identity. "And that means changing our mind forces us to reevaluate how we see ourselves and how we look at the world" (Lieberman, 2000:77).

The close-minded person *is* his position. His position is related to who he is or some other "deep" value. We have levels of values, some of which are more important than others. A deep value is one that helps define who we are. It tells us what we will and won't do. The fact that this type of stubborn person's values or core beliefs are at issue is to our advantage because values register physiological responses. Remember values and core beliefs, by definition, have emotional charge. Consequently, something that makes you feel bad is indicative of a value. Strong values are revealed by people's behaviors. Highly visual people exhibit the subtlest signs; mostly expressing their displeasure on their faces, especially around the eyes. They will raise and eyebrow, squint, and sometimes grimace. Auditories audibly often make audible noises. They sigh in exasperation or make sounds indicating their surprise or disgust. Kinesthetics will move their whole bodies. They might flinch, slap their thigh in annoyance, or shake their heads. They are often the easiest to read and if the value is deep enough most people will express their discomfort kinesthetically.

Deep values and core beliefs are part of who we are. The key to dealing with this form of resistance is to merge his self-concept with the behavior you are advocating. Changing the frame of the situation to include the behavior, thereby making it acceptable, even necessary, accomplishes this. Lieberman talks about the value against killing another person. Most of us believe that good people do not kill other people. Yet, some of us consider it permissible in defense of our life or the life of a loved one. Under these circumstances you can kill and still maintain your self-image of being a good person. The secret is to align yourself with a deeper and more important value to which this person adheres (Lieberman, 2000).

Hans Bleiker and his wife Annemarie have spent years examining value systems as they pertain to decision making (Hans' doctorate was in decision making theory at MIT). He cites at least four levels of values (Blieker and Bleiker, 1986). The most superficial are object-related values or values about taste and aesthetics. The next level is composed of process-related values or values about justice and fairness. The next level of values are meta-values or values about values. The first of these deep values being values that define rights, freedoms, and liberties. Bleiker explains that deep values provide common ground for conflict resolution. Although it may be possible for us to define even deeper values, for our purposes the deepest level of values address issues of personal responsibilities and limits on individual action (the fourth level). Bleiker's hierarchy of values is useful in two ways. First, it makes it possible to determine the values inherent to a proposal that may be problematic to your audience; and second, it makes it possible to identify the next lowest level of values where an agreement can be formed. It is important to note that we can reprioritize lesser values, but the deepest values do not offer us such opportunities. For example, environmentalists involved in a policy negotiation were willing to accept an outcome that involved more mercantile activities than they had originally supported because they considered the negotiation process to be fair (Mangin, 1989).

Another culture model allows me to predict the deep values of people on the basis of the social institutions they find critical. Irrespective of the country people come from, they tend to see the world as a marketplace, a community, or an association or corporation. Each of these social arrangements conditions us to have core beliefs about how things operate, our roles, and what we should do. These beliefs affect values and beliefs about processes, rights, and responsibilities.

A few years ago, I was asked to bring together a combative Information Technology community at a regional utility as a precursor to the introduction of an enterprise system (a software system that integrates all operations within a company). Each of the representatives had a reason to maintain their own little fiefdom and find some reason why they would not play an active role in the design of enterprise system requirements. Past efforts to consolidate operations or create uniform rules had failed or been complicated by efforts to retain idiosyncratic field codes, off-line subroutines, and patches that made subsystems work but created a cascade of unappreciated effects on others. After days of interaction, the most recalcitrant person in the room explicitly agreed to participate actively in the integration efforts. His change of heart was critical to the eventual fairly smooth implementation of an enterprise system. Everyone knew he had the most to lose by participating since he was not only capable, but had been and could continue to operate autonomously. His department operated on UNIX and he was the guru of the system, while everyone else had Microsoft and Oracle based systems. When he declared his willingness to participate, he acknowledged that he enjoyed his position as a rebel but that he saw value in this enterprise. Although he never gave more of an explanation, I think that several factors were involved in his decision. On an object-related level, he saw that e-mail connections and the electronic transmission of documents between his organization and others within and outside of the organization would be considerably easy if he were integrated into the system. But on a deeper level, his process-related values were being satisfied in the negotiations about system requirements. Participants were not allowed to withhold vital information or use their rank and organizational clout to manipulate the situation for departmental gains at the expense of others. In other words, everyone in the sessions had put their cards on the table, his opinion and those of others were equally respected and considered in deliberations, and he saw the real opportunity for the company to function like a community instead of an amalgamation of fiefdoms. The last point seemed to resonate with him a great deal, since he was the head of IT for the department of environment, fish and wildlife in the company. People earnestly involved in environmental affairs generally have a deep appreciation of community. After all, that's what an ecosystem is, and anyone who values communities accepts constraints on his or her personal freedoms in favor of measures to sustain the community to which they belong. He subordinated his need for independence for the opportunity to help his department to become more fully integrated into the organization. It is unlikely that he would articulate the same motives for his actions if someone were to interview him. This reflects one of the most interesting dimensions of values. You are generally unaware of them, until someone violates them; and the deeper the value, the less likely you know what troubles you about a situation. It's like having a deep pain, it is hard to explain where it is coming from, but you know it's there and that you must act to alleviate it.

Persuading people who are resistant to an idea they perceive to be inconsistent with their self-concept does not require the fabrication of a reason for acting. The main objective is to present the idea in the appropriate manner assuming that the idea has intrinsic worth. Here, the reason is not as important as the presentation. You must present the idea in a way that incorporates your desire into his idea of virtue and how he sees himself. "Instead of trying to overcome his sense of decency, you simply appeal to it" (Lieberman, 2000:78).

A few nonverbal principles generally apply when you are dealing with resistance. Since physiology affects emotions, affecting someone's physiology affects their emotional state. Resistance is a form of emotional rigidity, so physical movement causes a corresponding emotional movement.

Surprisingly, the first law of motion affects people. This law states that, "a body remains at rest or, if already in motion, remains in uniform motion with constant speed (well, maybe not constant) in a straight line, unless it is acted on by an unbalanced external force" (Asimov, 1966:24). The following nonverbal principle is derived from this rule.

Tip #11: Once people move, they are predisposed to continue to move in the same direction.

You can be the external force (hopefully not unbalanced) that sets people in motion if you can get people to bend or move their bodies. Once they move, they are inclined to continue to move in the same direction. In other words, once people change their minds either to lower or raise their expectations, they are inclined to do it again. This is a version of the idea of the "slippery slope."

Tip #12: People respond reflexively to nonverbal directions.

You can initiate or maintain movement without asking. People will move, if you move with confidence. For example, if you get up and move to the window without making eye contact, they will feel inclined to move. If you want to test this idea, simply look up in a public place and stare at the ceiling for a few minutes. Within minutes people will feel compelled to look up and you will not have had to say anything.

Surprise is generally a wonderful thing, but in a negotiation it is often a problem. It takes you out of your game momentarily and can cause you to talk to yourself while in front of someone. There is an old rule in negotiation that says, "Never negotiate with yourself in front of others." This is sound advice. When you start to talk to yourself, you go "inside of yourself" and lose track of what is going on in your environment. This is the perfect time for someone unscrupulous to talk about important details or shut you down when you are attempting to acquire something.

Auditories typically remember listening to something particularly interesting and within moments finding themselves engaged in a deep internal dialogue. By the time you returned from your "trip," the lecturer was talking about something different and you had no idea of how he got there. Imagine this happening in a negotiation. It does, and it can be a serious problem if it happens at the wrong time.

You can shift people into an auditory mode by giving them a reason to remember something that was said earlier or by getting them to recall two different perspectives of an argument. Once in this mode, they are distractible and become more susceptible to new ideas.

Key #3

It's not what you say; but what you do that counts.

Make My Day!

"When nonverbal and verbal cues seem to contradict each other, a listener-perceiver will usually trust the nonverbals" (Brilhart, 1986:198). This generality applies to most people, but trained interviewers pay specific attention to nonverbal cues not consciously controlled or monitored by the sender. These nonverbal signals are controlled by the basal structures of the brain such as the hypothalamus, brain stem, pineal gland, and other parts of the brain that control bodily processes, hormone outputs, and feelings. These nonverbal signals are subject to little or no conscious control. For example, we have little control over whether we sweat or not, whether our blood pressure rises or declines, or whether we blush or stutter. Changes in muscle tension, pupil size, micro-expressions occur automatically in response to situations. Even body parts that we normally control such as our feet, the set of our head, and our posture can betray us when we focus on other things. Interrogators count on this phenomenon to detect deception because people cannot avoid communicating nonverbally.

When Clint Eastwood as Dirty Harry says, "Make my day" to a street criminal, most people don't have to guess that he is making a threat. How do we know this? We know because our brains have quickly processed a great deal of nonverbal information including the context of the situation, facial expressions, body posture, tone, and voice qualities. In an instant, we have noted the slight grimace on Dirty Harry's face, the coldness of his gaze, the raspy quality of his voice, and the overall tension in his body. These cues lead us to conclude that his statement is meant to be menacing – even when we can't see his rather large gun. This skill is critical to our survival and is highlighted in stressful situations.

When determining meaning in situations that are new, emotional, or difficult, we typically assume that what you say is not as informative as what your body does. These situations stimulate our physiology in ways that sensitize us to nonverbal cues – sometimes at the expense of our capacity to appreciate talk. Perhaps our reliance on nonverbal cues is a reflection of the fact that language is a relatively new invention and we have over a hundred thousand years of experience reading nonverbal behavior in threatening situations. Anyway, deriving more of the meaning in the situation from unconscious nonverbal behavior makes sense since it is harder to lie with your body than your mouth. The object of our attention sends signals unconsciously. Their body position, facial expression, muscle tone, voice characteristics, and gaze behavior are all processed almost simultaneously and mostly unconsciously. We become aware of an impression – for example, whether we like or trust a person – but not the process that creates the impression. Our impressions come to us as a gestalt (an impression presented as a whole that cannot easily be explained through the analysis of its parts). In these situations, we often cannot explain how we arrived at a conclusion, but we know how we *feel* about the subject.

The fact that we *feel* the conclusion suggests that the right hemisphere of the brain does the information processing. The right hemisphere is known to process nonverbal cues and feelings (Hampton-Turner, 1981). Its processes are much different than the left hemisphere's linear and verbal processes. Right hemisphere processing involves the simultaneous assessment and synthesis of data acquired in three dimensions. It is quick, oriented toward emotional cues, highly intuitive, and operates below our level of conscious awareness.

Right hemisphere processing is part of what makes subliminal influence using fixed action patterns (FAPs) possible. The behaviors demonstrated in these patterns are almost always the same and produced in the same order. Cialdini (1984) compares these patterns of behaviors to recorded tapes in the animal kingdom. Actions that represent parts of provocative situations trigger complex responses in people and animals. "Horse whisperers" use this phenomenon to manage horses humanely. For example, they might make clawing movements in the air toward a horse to simulate an attack by a big cat and trigger a startle response. These movements triggers a flight response in the horse as it tries to escape the threat. When the horse finds that it cannot escape, it eventually decides to accept the "horse whisperer" as its leader and becomes submissive. Using refined nonverbal behavior in this way allows the "horse whisperer" to tame the horse without "breaking" its spirit.

Neither people nor animals are responding to the whole situation in a FAP. A specific feature in an interaction activates pre-programmed tapes and our behaviors become automatic. Anyone who has children and catches herself doing what she said that she would never do because she hated it when her mom did it, understands this idea. The tape just pops into place and a standard sequence of behaviors become automatic. "Although they usually work to our advantage, the trigger features that activate [the tapes] can be used to dupe us into playing them at the wrong times" (Cialdini, 1984:4).

Eye movements, for example, trigger automatic behaviors and thoughts. If you get into an elevator and look straight up, after a while you will notice everyone looking at the ceiling. They won't know why but they will feel compelled to look. Eye behavior can also trigger ideas. For instance, if you use a word that expresses displeasure while looking at a person they will assume that you are talking about them.

Fixed-action patterns can also be triggered by breathing rates and voice patterns. If you sit next to someone who has labored breathing, you will find your stress levels increasing. A relaxed breather can have the opposite effect on people. Similarly, a shrill human voice can make people uneasy, while a soft mellifluous voice relaxes people and puts them at ease.

You're Part of the Presentation

It is important to understand how people see you to determine how to most effectively frame your proposal or argument. In other words, your image should be taken into consideration when framing your argument or proposal. Your position on an issue can be seen as credible or weak depending on how you are perceived. It is also important to note that you are not necessarily stuck with your image. For example, think about Fred Grandy, the former Midwestern congressman. I am pretty sure that he downplayed his role as "Gopher" on the Love Boat when he campaigned for Congress and played up the fact that he was a Rhodes scholar. Similarly, Senator Fred Thompson from Tennessee has made reference to the fact that he was an attorney in interviews, but rarely talked about his career as an actor. Yet, I would be surprised if he wouldn't mention it if the senate was dealing with a bill about the movie industry.

Your image should be consistent with your message and goal. The most notable example of a politician who paid a heavy price for not thinking about the impact of image on credibility is former presidential candidate Michael Dukakis. Some people believe that he lost the election to George Bush because of how he answered correspondent Bernard Shaw's question about the death penalty. Dukakis was against the death penalty, but when he was asked whether he would maintain his position if the convicted person had killed his wife, he disregarded what his handlers had told him and answered the question as framed. The sad thing is that he could have maintained his view that the death penalty was immoral and not injured his image as a candidate if he had explained that it wasn't a hypothetical situation for him. A close relative of his had been murdered, the killer had been caught and he had not supported the death penalty in that case. Explaining this to the American public would have left many people with the impression that he was a man of his conviction, instead of a passionless policy wonk. Dukakis' answer reinforced his negative image as a technocrat and may have cost him the presidency. Always think about your goal and ask yourself if the image that you are projecting in trying to attain it aids or hinders you.

Impressions of images stay in the audience's mind longer than well-crafted words. Use your words to create the image you desire by framing the situation. Had Dukakis explained that the situation was not hypothetical, he would have reframed the question in such a way that would have allowed him to express his view on the issue, made connection with people's emotions, *and* shown him to be a man of conviction. That would have been a "home run." You can modify or reinforce an image in moments with a good introductory comment before answering a question.

Dukakis had an opportunity to take advantage of an auditory fixed action pattern (FAP). People, especially those in rapport, can feel a speaker-sender's emotions as they talk. Mr. Dukakis failed to take the opportunity to engender sympathy and highlight his personableness while making his point. All he had to do was tell his story while reliving the events in his mind. His voice would naturally have reflected his emotions and would have allowed him to establish an emotional connection with his audience that would have moved them.

In addition to projecting the right image, credibility can be enhanced or damaged by the delivery of a message. Someone short like Michael Dukakis had to be concerned about projecting an image of strength since people generally think of short people as weak. The image of Michael Dukakis in an oversized tank helmet, with his head bobbing like pop up toy, certainly did not help his presidential prospects. In contrast, consider Mr. Putin, the president of Russia who is also not a big man. It is probably not an accident that his press people emphasized the fact that he was formerly a big guy in the KGB. This highlights an important fact – image often has both a positive and a negative side. In this case, the positives about KGB affiliation probably outweighed the negative. The Russian people wanted a strong leader so they might return to their days as a Superpower. The affiliation with the KGB made him look strong and brought back memories of the days when Russia was strong. The fact that the KGB was oppressive was all but disregarded by the people, although the mobsters operating in the country were probably concerned. It is also not an accident that the Russian press highlighted the fact that Mr. Putin has a black belt in judo. Again, his advisors helped him reinforce an image of strength and discipline.

Both Mr. Dukakis and Mr. Putin's images were greatly affected by a kinesthetic FAP. People who are still and maintain an erect posture nonverbally convey a sense of confidence and authority to others, and people react to them accordingly. Images of Dukakis' head bobbing up and down uncontrollably as he rode in the tank greatly undermined his authority and appearance of being in control.

Mr. Putin's image actually benefits from his appearance on television. Even though he like Dukakis is a fairly short man, he wears dark pinstripes (thus making him look large if not tall) and he moves erectly and with balance, while keeping his head relatively still. His smooth, coordinated gait, no doubt partially the result of his training in judo, conveys power, authority and agility.

People who understand how to manipulate their image often have great concern about being seen with the right people. This is particularly important in organizational hierarchies. It is conventional wisdom that you have to look the part to get the job. This is often true. Being seen with "big people" increases your likelihood of being thought of as a "big person."

Stand and Deliver

Credibility can also be enhanced by good delivery; and good delivery requires discipline in making proposals and arguments. Always think about your goal; it should inform what you say and do. For example, if you need to establish your credibility find a way to stand. It is easier to establish credibility while positioned above an audience's head level than below or at their level. There is a kinesthetic fixed action pattern at work here and it is one of the reasons why a dais is elevated and judges are seated the way they are in courtrooms.

How you stand is also important. Being still with your weight distributed evenly between both feet conveys authority. Many people actually undermine their authority as they lean on chairs, against walls, or on a podium while talking. These actions subliminally suggest to your audience that you are weak. Trying to be assertive while leaning on something sends a mixed message that does not work in your favor.

In many speeches, President Bush can be seen awkwardly leaning on a podium as he tries to be presidential. It appears that his handlers are trying to strike a balance between being authoritative and being amiable. His leaning accomplishes neither. Although putting more weight on one foot and moving in a relaxed manner tends to subliminally convey friendliness, using the right hand and the voice to be assertive cancels the effect.

You've Got 30 Seconds

Image is critical in high-level politics, and it is often presented in 30-second increments. Politicians are forced to commit to a goal (or subgoal) that can be attained in 30 seconds. They have to design their message delivery to be television friendly. It has to be short (or be editable into a 30 second blurb), appeal to the eye, and still send a powerful message.

The 30-second target is a little unrealistic in real life, but it does discipline a speaker to think about pacing and maintaining an audience's attention and energy. Crafting a message to have periodic mini-climaxes every 30 seconds is a good idea. These mini-climaxes can be structured around short-term and ultimate goals. Short-term goals are the words or actions that keep your listeners moving toward your ultimate goal; and the ultimate goal is the set of words or actions that once said or done eliminate the need for further persuasion.

Every audience has four major concerns when you appear in front of them according to Michael Shadow (1988). First, they want to know that you know what you are talking about. Second, they want to know whether they can trust you (i.e., are you safe, honest, friendly, or kind). Third, they want to know if you have their best interests at heart. And finally, they want to know whether you have the energy to pursue their interests. Each of these four questions can be a short-term goal addressed by your message and its delivery.

The nonverbals of authority and confidence predispose people to think that you are competent. People don't trust others until they feel safe, and the human voice is one of the best tools for creating safety. This is an auditory FAP that seems to start in infancy as mother's coo and rock agitated babies to soothe them. Grown up children and adults are still prone to experience a sense of safety when listening to a calm, relaxed voice. Conversely, tension and stress in a speaker's voice creates anxiety in an audience and undermines its confidence in the speaker.

Different audiences evaluate earnestness in different ways. While there are no nonverbals directly related to earnestness, congruence tends to give the impression of earnestness. On the other hand, nonverbal behavior that seems to contradict verbal messages erodes people's belief in the earnestness of a speaker.

The last major concern is clearly associated with nonverbal behavior. People who appear sluggish or lethargic subconsciously send messages that suggest a lack of dynamism. The hidden assumption in operation is that dynamic people are dynamic. That is, their gestures are crisp, they walk with authority, and they appear to have stamina. Overweight people generally do not appear to be dynamic, unless they are also big. Sports commentator Mike Madden is a good example of someone whose still photo might not project dynamism, but through the use of his voice and gestures creates the impression of dynamism. Whether intentional or not, he uses auditory and kinesthetic FAPs to create excitement and to connect with his audiences.

Incongruity can be Deceptive

People assess your attitude from your posture, gesture, and especially, tone of voice relative to a situation. Threat or danger is intuitively detected in the quality of the voice. Few people interpret Dirty Harry's "Make my day!" statement as anything but a threat. In fact, the recognition of this statement as a threat comes from the fact that the words, and the facial expression and voice are incongruous.

Incongruity can also be skillfully manipulated to induce apprehension or fear. Muhammad Ali was able to demoralize Smokin' Joe Frazier in one of their epic battles after Frazier hit him so hard, as he put it, "my grandfather felt it." Frazier knew that he had to have hurt him badly, but began doubting himself when Ali pulled him close and calmly whispered, "Is that all you got, Joe?" Ali's behavior was not in alignment with what Frazier expected of someone hit that hard. The difference between Ali's demeanor and the expected effect of the punch, and then the incongruity of Ali's comment, introduced doubt into Frazier's mind. This doubt, and maybe fear, allowed Ali to survive the round and eventually win the fight.

People intrinsically have the ability to detect anxiety and stress in a human voice. If you don't believe me, approach a toddler and talk to them like you are under duress. Many little children will start to cry. They know something is wrong.

The Four Ps

Nonverbal communication can be thought of in terms of four Ps: pace, priorities, presentation, and packaging. There is potential conflict whenever people's expectations of the four Ps don't match what they experience. Pace is about tempo. People think, speak and act at different speeds. For example, visual processing of information is the fastest and kinesthetic processing is the slowest. People who talk too fast induce stress in other people. Conversely, people who talk to slowly induce ennui.

People with different priorities are destined to be in conflict. From a communications perspective, priorities are expressed in terms of what comes first in a conversation, what people talk about the most, or what they emphasize. Someone whose favorite topic is himself rarely holds an audience for very long and tends not to be very accommodating.

Presentation refers to the way something is performed in terms of the use of voice, gestures, visual material, or props. It includes style, dynamism, and sometimes, even deference and demeanor.

The last "P" is packaging and involves the way the message is put together. Issues of structure such as orderliness, aesthetics and sequencing are aspects of packaging.

Receiving information in ways that are not compatible with our preferred way of communicating or thinking increases our uneasiness and perception of risk. For example, a violation of "pace" can produce more than just boredom. It can produce confusion, and confusion causes people to rely on their basic assumptions about people's motivation and intention. As a result, they tend to withhold or distort information, and become resistant to change by rejecting proposals before thinking about them. The operating rule for most people when confused seems to be "better safe than sorry."

Bodily Influence

If my goal is to acquire information, I'd like the speaker to be in an auditory state. They are easier to talk with and more likely to disclose information. When people are comfortable, it is not unusual for them to shift into an auditory state. Your job if you commit to gathering information is to help them make that shift. Once there, they have a tendency to talk too much if you get them excited. But in this state, they are prone to divulge more than is strategically prudent.

Proxemics are an important nonverbal means of encouraging auditory processing. Auditory people need to be close enough to be able to whisper to you. This spacing allows them to use their full repertoire of voice patterns. They tend to lean forward to express interest or make points as they talk to you. Leaning toward them is a nonverbal sign of interest and makes them feel comfortable.

You can encourage auditory behavior by bobbing your head rhythmically (an auditory FAP) and offering nonverbal forms of acknowledgement like "uh huh," "tell me more," or other short comments about what is being said. Do not worry about waiting for the person to stop talking, auditories don't mind talking at the same time as another person, especially when that person is affirming or acknowledging what they say.

Auditories appreciate enthusiasm and emotional intensity in your voice. An organized talk in which a speaker enunciates clearly and calmly appeals to them a great deal. A varied and well-modulated voice is mesmerizing to them, especially if the presentation is full of detailed descriptions and elaborations.

It is important to allow enough time for an interview with an auditory. It will almost always take more time than necessary to cover the topic if they feel comfortable with you. Auditories are natural storytellers and they enjoy an attentive audience. A Proctor and Gamble manager interviewed me for a sales position in my senior year of college. Early in the interview, he noted my background in linguistics and asked me if I knew anything about the Samoan language. I told him that I didn't know anything about it, but that I did know a few Samoan football players. He then gave me the proper pronunciation of the name of our star running back and told me that he was one of 10,000 non-native speakers of the language. The interview lasted an hour and was very entertaining. At its end, he looked at me and said, "I've really enjoyed this interview, but I now realize that you know a lot about me, and I know very little about you." Apparently he knew enough to recommend me for the fourth and final interview in their process. You can form a bond with an auditory by just being an attentive listener. Repeat what they say, ask follow-up questions, and give them time. Time is "relationship" for auditories. They do not like to be rushed through their stories. They can be very informative because they naturally provide context for their stories and are patient about explaining background information. Your apparent interest stimulates their willingness to talk.

Auditories tend to be very literal. If you ask sloppy questions, the interview will be of limited value. They admire precision in language and that means appropriate vocabulary, logic, and enunciation. If you mumble as you talk to an auditory, you are likely to induce stress or make them disinterested in talking to you.

Auditories also react to the quality of your voice. A mellifluous voice can be mesmerizing to an auditory person. These are the people who love Julie Andrews, Demi Moore and Sigourney Weaver because of their voices.

The movie "My Fair Lady" highlights the importance of language to auditory cultures. Social status is determined by language skills in British, French, and even German culture.

Visual people tend to want the most distance between you and them. They feel comfortable speaking to you from a distance beyond your arm length. They don't need to be close; they want to see you. If you get too close to them, they become self-conscious.

Posture is important to visual people. They are apt to interpret slouching negatively. They may interpret it as a sign of disinterest or disrespect, which can result in a shortened interview. Visuals also tend to move very little as they speak and they tend not to like too much movement from others. They can become agitated or annoyed by people who fidget or make large hand gestures. Visuals like tight, contained movements.

Crisp, direct questions or statements are preferred by visuals. They are very conscious of time and will cut an interview short if they think that you are likely to waste their time by meandering or stammering. They expect people to speak clearly, concisely and get to the point.

Visuals prefer to start with a broad overview of a topic, and then to "drill down." They like people who are prepared. Presentations featuring graphics, slides, or graphs give this impression and satisfy their interest in "eye candy."

Kinesthetic people are very different than visual people. They tend to want to have personal interactions at close range. Once they are comfortable with someone, they tend to want to interact at a distance that allows them to touch the other person.

Kinesthetics can learn a lot about you from a handshake. They get a feel for your honesty, confidence, strength and commitment, among other things. A weak handshake can start a conversation off on the wrong foot. The conclusion they draw depends on situational factors and is often interpreted at gut level. For example, a weak handshake without eye contact to finalize a deal can actually kill the deal.

Tactile kinesthetics (generally males) tend not to like much eye contact, but not when shaking hands. In other circumstances, they will often stand or sit shoulder-to-shoulder so that they can have minimal eye contact yet be close to another person.

Kinesthetics want to be active in interactions. Hands-on activities really appeal to them. In fact, almost anything that involves audience participation is appealing. They enjoy props that they can touch and opportunities to interact with others in workshops. When presenting to them, allocate time for unexpected questions and objections. It is also wise to allow time for breaks because they get antsy.

The pause is one of the most powerful aspects of nonverbal communication. Its meaning depends on the context in which it occurs. For example, it can be interpreted to mean that you appreciate the gravity of a situation, that you are deliberating, or that you are contemplating taking action. Pay close attention to how long you pause, what you appear to be doing while you are pausing; but most of all, pay attention to what they do while you pause.

A well-timed pause is an opportunity to observe people's behavior without being conspicuous. It allows you to see someone's reaction to a proposal so that you can measure its effect.

Key #4

If the eyes are the windows of the soul, then bodies are the windows of thoughts and feelings.

You Can Run, But You Can't Hide

Every time you talk to someone you send at least one verbal and one nonverbal message to him or her. Sometimes the messages match, that is to say, both messages convey the same thought; and sometimes they don't. When the messages don't match, we call them incongruous. Incongruous messages are common in conflicts. For example, people will be visibly upset yet when asked what troubles them, they say, "nothing." How do we know that they are not being candid? We know because we note the incongruity between what their nonverbal behavior was "saying" and what they said verbally. This incongruity is not necessarily "body language" in terms of gestures. It is what people's facial expressions, voices, stiffness, and skin color tells us is going on.

Controlling involuntary gestures requires a mastery of body control that few people can hope to attain. Generally, the best we can do is to reduce the visibility or frequency of nonverbal behaviors like blinking, squinting, or frowning. Nonverbal behaviors including changes in muscle tension, skin color, and voice qualities are controlled by the part of our nervous system generally beyond our conscious control. If you pay attention to the physical changes exhibited by the body of a speaker (or a listener) *and* the verbal content (what they say), you will obtain information about what they are thinking and feeling.

Two characteristics of nonverbal communication are extremely valuable to communicators. First, it is impossible to prevent your body from sending these messages; and second, the majority of significant nonverbal behaviors are universal. In other words, if you're a human, you are physiologically "wired" to respond to appealing or threatening stimuli in the same way that everyone else does. You may respond more quickly or more visibly, but these are only differences of degree not category.

A wide range of nonverbal behaviors is encompassed by our "fight, flight, fright" physiological response. Although the "fight or flight response" is anachronistic, we experience it many times a week. It is a constant reminder that humans are *feeling* more than thinking creatures (Damasio, 1994). Our fight or flight response evolved to enable us to survive physical threats from predators; and it persists. In an encounter with a beast, having the strength to fend it off or run with great speed could save your life. Unfortunately, your body responds to symbolic threats like obstacles to satisfying your needs or attaining goals in the same way it responds to a physical threat. Since you rarely have the opportunity to convert the burst of energy that your body produces in a workplace setting, you are left dealing with a lot of internal energy some of which your body converts to external signals. Many such signals are sent in social conflicts and negotiations.

The energy in your body is a source of information to anyone who pays close attention to you. It drives your physiology; and your physiology reveals the presence of emotions and thoughts in ways that are sometimes obvious, and at other times, subtle. There is little you can do to prevent someone reading you like a book, unless you're a master yogi.

Not only does our body betray what is going on inside of us emotionally, it also tells an attentive observer a lot about what we are thinking about and how we are thinking about it. Muscles become tense and skin becomes red or pale as thoughts and feelings course through us.

Tip# 17: People's willingness to allow you to ask questions, and their willingness to respond with candor is revealed by regular, deep breathing.

The connection between the mind and the body make it possible for communications researchers to come to the following conclusions (Leathers, 1992).

1. Feelings and emotions are more accurately expressed nonverbally than verbally.
2. The nonverbal portion of communication conveys meanings and intentions that are relatively free of deception and distortion.
3. Nonverbal cues provide the intention and motivation underlying messages that are indispensable in attaining high quality communication.

Move the Body, Move the Mind

You learn about the world through your body via your senses and you express what is happening in your body through movement. People trying to influence you have access to four main "channels" of communication – what you see, what you hear, what you feel (the process) and what you think (the content). When they successfully manage these channels, they literally "move you." The outward expression of internal sensations ranges from tiny and unconscious movements – the corners of your mouth turn down or your head nods slightly, to large and conscious gestures.

> "People reading is possible because our minds and our bodies are so connected that we cannot change one without changing the other" (Slater, 1993:32).

It is almost impossible to change your mind without changing your body. Poker players and high stakes negotiators count on this. New cards or new assessments of situations induce changes in your body.

There are also changes in the body required to change from listening to the environment to scanning the environment visually. As you change the focus of your attention from one channel to another, your body also changes. The changes can be detected in the way we use our eyes and voice as well as the way we breathe.

Each of the four primary channels of communication is associated with specific physiological states. Each channel actually demands certain types of bodily changes to influence perception. These can be seen as fixed action patterns since changing body position produces reflexive changes in thinking and perceiving. For example, in order to use your visual channel you will find yourself adjusting your posture to be more upright. Straightening your back raises your head and allows you to see more. "The higher the tower, the better the view." Holding your body in an upright position requires that you tighten your torso. A tight torso means that your diaphragm has less room to move and, you will exhibit shallow or "high breathing." When you have less air in your lungs, you have less oxygen in your body, and the blood flow to your limbs and extremities is reduced. Your skin color reflects this lack of blood flow as pale skin. Additionally, vocal chords tighten to permit the production of more words with less air. Tight vocal chords also result in a high-pitched voice and fast rate of speed (Slater (1993).

As you focus on hearing to listen to something like music, you relax your posture allowing you to breathe more deeply. Since you're getting more air, you can relax your vocal chords and exercise more control of your rate of speech and pitch giving you a richer, deeper voice. This is the reason why singers and woodwind musicians are trained to breathe deeper. The ample supply of air in your body allows your peripheral circulation to increase and your skin becomes slightly flushed.

To feel requires even more relaxation than hearing. To be aware of your feelings, you must breathe deeply and relax. You oxygenate your nervous system and draw in more air than is necessary for speech. As a result of the change in your breathing, your voice becomes deep, and even breathy. Exhalations are frequently audible as excess air escaping makes "h" and "s" sounds. A noticeable blush indicates that your body is well oxygenated. As you focus on your feelings, you can actually feel your skin warming up.

The fourth channel, digital thinking, reflects thought without emotion and is necessary for doing calculations, recalling facts, and pondering theory. It is not related to a sensory system and is a recent evolutionary development in humans. It has been described as a very narrow state of consciousness because it is so difficult to maintain. Maintaining this state of consciousness requires that you freeze your body and assume a rigid posture. The effect, of course, is to make your breathing shallow again. As a result of your body's effort to conserve air, your rate of speech increases and your voice becomes monotone and flat. This is of little concern since your attention in this mental state is focused on the meaning of words and you would not want to risk distorting it with inflection. The low level of air available in your extremities makes your skin turn pale (Slater, 1993).

The "Eyes" Have It

Our eyes serve many vitally important communication functions. In particular, they have a wide range of nonverbal impacts. Leathers (1992:57) reports that the eyes:

1. indicate degrees of attentiveness, interest, and arousal
2. help initiate and sustain intimate relationships
3. influence attitude change and persuasion
4. regulate interaction
5. communicate emotions
6. define power and status relationships
7. assume a central role in impression management

The functions of most interest to us include: the attention function, the persuasive function, the regulatory function, the power function, and the affective function. With regard to the attention function, eyes signal a readiness to communicate. People are consciously aware of your eye behavior. They tend to interpret your willingness to make eye contact as willingness to listen when they want to talk. Your eye behavior can indicate your level of interest or that you want to get someone's attention.

Your eyes can be used to acquire someone's attention. It is common for people in stores and in restaurants to seek assistance by making eye contact with service providers.

When talking to someone, listeners assume that eye contact is an indication of whether or not you are paying attention to them. I once watched a strange "dance" between an auditory senior executive who liked to close his eyes to concentrate during a briefing and a man giving a report. When the executive closed his eyes in the meeting (there were others in attendance), the briefer would stop talking. When he stopped talking, the executive would roll his head forward and open his eyes looking in the direction of the briefer, and then the man would start to talk. Once he started to talk the executive would close his eyes and the whole "dance" would start again. Many people will stop talking when you stop looking at them.

The pupils of the eyes grow large when a person is aroused. Any form of arousal can potentially increase their size, researchers have even found a correlation between the degree of a person's sexual arousal and pupil size. The pupils of heterosexual individuals were observed to dilate when they view the nude body of the opposite sex (Leathers, 1992).

As further proof that arousal is the issue, not sex, pupil size also increases as the cognitive difficulty of a reading task increases. It also increases as the level of interest in anything increases. Both of these observations can be useful in watching a light-eyed person reading a contract or receiving a proposal.

The pupils of the eye also enlarge when someone experiences positive emotions such as happiness and joy, and they contract when someone experiences sadness or sorrow. "The eyes accurately reflect whether a person is experiencing a positive or negative emotion and reveal the intensity of the emotion . . . We display the kind of emotions we are experiencing in our face and the intensity of the emotion in our eyes" (Leathers, 1992:62).

Related to the belief that someone making eye contact is paying attention to you is the belief that eye contact indicates your level of interest in something. My fairness has been questioned by a party involved in mediation solely on the basis of the impression that I looked at the other party more than them. When asked if the agreement seemed unfair they said it didn't, but it was clear that they had subjected it to a high level of scrutiny because of the impression my eye behavior had made.

Persuasive power seems to be directly related to eye behavior in many people. Although the following statement is probably truer of visual people, research indicates that, "the persuader who wishes to be perceived as credible must sustain eye contact while speaking and being spoken to by the listener-perceiver. To avoid a marked decline in their credibility, persuasive communicators must not be shifty-eyed, look down or away from the listener-perceiver frequently, blink excessively, or exhibit eye-flutter" (Leathers, 1992:59).

Eyes regulate interactions by alerting a listener-perceiver that we want to hold the floor. Direct eye contact can tell a listener that we are still thinking and talking. Conversely, it can tell a speaker when a listener is about to speak.

There is growing evidence that gaze behavior combined with gestures serve to effectively communicate the turn-maintaining, turn-yielding, turn-requesting, and turn-taking cues that are central to managing conversations. They represent a subtle and less assertive way to reveal a person's inclination to talk or listen.

Another conventional nonverbal aspect of eye behavior of interest to us has to do with the eyes' ability to communicate emotion. Eyes, in combination with the face, function as a powerful medium for communicating feelings. It is difficult to get a party to feel sympathy for someone with cold or hateful eyes.

The last conventional aspect of eye behavior to be discussed here is the power function. The eyes play a central role in establishing dominance and submissiveness. They are an effective and reliable index of the amount of power one individual possesses vis-à-vis another. People with power have license to stare at others for the purpose of domination. By contrast, eyes averted and looking downward are universally recognized as a sign of weakness and submission.

Eyes can also be used to regulate interactions. Someone perceived to have power who stares at someone who is misbehaving can often cause them to stop, especially if that stare is accompanied by a demonstrative hand gesture. Many fathers, including mine used to stop me from misbehaving by staring at me.

Eyes Can Talk

The eyes answer what and how, and sometimes who, questions. The way people move their eyes is very informative to a skilled observer. Watching where they direct their attention can tell you who or what they think is important in an interaction. For instance, many complex negotiations involve teams of negotiators each with slightly different interests or representing a different part of an organization. It is often possible to know whose interests are at stake by watching to see where members of the other side direct their attention when you address specific issues or interests. People often cannot help looking at people whom they know control, or have strong interests, in an issue. Why waste time trying to convince someone who is only marginally interested? Watching them tells you who among them needs to be persuaded. Information about which issues are important and to whom, can be invaluable when trying to get the other side to negotiate about priorities.

People commonly believe that someone whose eyes move a great deal when interacting with others is shifty. This may or may not be true. Nervousness will cause people to scan the environment, especially if the person is overwhelmed or anticipating something unpleasant.

Most interrogators are trained to note when people make and break eye contact. If you break eye contact to make a statement, many interrogators will assume that your answer is less than truthful. They also note how you move your eyes because they can be used to determine whether someone is making up an answer to a question or remembering an answer. Most people move their eyes horizontally and to the right to remember what they have heard and in the opposite direction to fabricate an answer.

Sometimes the fact that eyes are not moving is important. If you pay close attention, you will notice that some people's eyes will remain motionless for short periods of time. This is often a sign that the person is visualizing something. People in this state are not very aware of what is going on around them because they are temporarily preoccupied.

Eye movements also correspond to the way people have stored information in their brains. Paying close attention to a person's eyes while they discuss important issues can reveal how information has been stored and whether strong emotions are associated with the recalled events or thoughts.

Was it Something I Said?

There are several fixed action patterns associated with gaze behavior and eye movement. For example, people are predisposed to believe that anyone looking at them while saying something positive or negative is commenting about them.

Many of us have experienced someone taking offense at something not directed at them but said while looking at them. This experience is so common that it forms the basis for some situation comedies. For example, a wife will ask a naïve husband how her dress looks and he will look at the dress and not realizing that he is perceived to be looking at her say something like "It's kind of bland." She will then respond, "So, you think I'm bland!" and the interaction then degenerates into a fight. The audience laughs and tends to perceive her as being overly sensitive, or they think that the man should have said something nice instead of being so blunt. Saying something nice would not have accomplished his goal, if he wanted her to reconsider her choice of dresses. However, he could say exactly the same thing while looking toward the closet and she might even agree with him. She is less likely to think his comments are directed at her if he does not look at her. The wife is not being overly sensitive; she is being human. The error is not with the husband in saying what he felt, but in nonverbally assigning a negative label to his wife. People feel that you are talking about them when you look at them and define things as good or bad.

Tip #   14: Making judgments while looking at someone will give that person the impression that you are talking about him or her.

Professional interviewers, like mediators, commonly observe a visual FAP in the course of their interviews. Interviewers will pause and then look down during the interview. They do this to recall the feelings associated with an event. Some people will even close their eyes to increase their capacity to experience feelings or body sensations.

Visual FAPs are very valuable for managing two-way interactions. There are FAPs that encourage talk, stop talk, and create impressions about speaker-senders. One of these FAPs was alluded to earlier in a retail situation. In some circumstances, making eye contact encourages engagement. For example, if you make eye contact with a salesclerk and that salesclerk does not approach you, you are likely to interpret the clerk's behavior unfavorably.

Some FAPs are related to how people process information. For example, a facilitator who has just requested that members of a group be quiet can trigger speech from an auditory person by making eye contact with him or her, even after just having asked for quiet. In this context, auditory people with something to say often perceive eye contact by a facilitator as acknowledgement that they have the floor.

What Are You Looking At?

Most communication training asserts that listeners should make eye contact with a speaker. This is generally advisable, but not always. Some people find eye contact to be a major distraction, or even an annoyance.

It is important to note that we do not all listen in the same way. Our listening style depends on our lead system (visual, auditory, or kinesthetic). Don't let your listening style be an unnecessary source of conflict with a speaker. Differences in representational system preferences affect the nonverbal aspects of communications such as turn taking, gaze behavior, speaking distance, and repose. Most of us are unaware of differences in communication styles unless we are dealing with someone from a foreign culture. We are surprised to learn that we don't have to go overseas to encounter people with different rules concerning communication. Interestingly, the significance of these differences only becomes apparent to many of us when we marry into a family that communicates differently than our family does. Every family has its own rules about the use of emotion, volume, animation, and space when communicating.

The way people listen varies significantly. Some of us listen with our eyes and feel the need to fix our eyes on a speaker. We do not believe that we can truly listen without looking at a speaker, and we tend to believe that others are not listening to us unless they do the same. This need to focus our attention on a speaker can be problematic, especially when the listener is trying to describe his or her feelings or find the right words to express a complex idea. Fixing your eyes on a speaker trying to find words to describe feelings often makes it difficult for the speaker to produce smooth, flowing speech. Making eye contact in such situations actually interferes with a speaker's ability to use his brain. At that moment, the person being looked at experiences discomfort and feels inept, but does not know why.

The more emotional the topic is, the more the listener should consider breaking eye contact with a speaker. This can be done by periodically gazing toward the speaker and then down. Slowly directing our eyes downward while breathing slowly and deeply facilitates the speaker's ability to access their own feelings.

If you know that a topic is bound to elicit an emotional response, you might position yourself so that you are not facing the other party. You or the listener should either sit side-by-side with the speaker or at a 90-degree angle from him or her.

Tip #15: Avoid direct eye contact so people can process emotions.

Tip #16: People in an auditory state do not need eye contact and may find it distracting.

Tip #17: People in a visual state expect eye contact; otherwise they question your interest in what they are saying.

Tip #18: People in a kinesthetic state communicate more readily when you are close to them.

Negotiating with the Body

The most important nonverbal behaviors in negotiations indicate intransigence or a willingness to make concessions. Interestingly, the expressions we use to describe encounters give us clues about some of the behaviors to look for. A person who is not going to yield "stands firm," "sets his jaw," or "stiffens." People ready to fight prepare for it by creating a firm base from which to strike. They also make themselves appear larger as they tense their muscles. In the animal world, these actions warn other animals to back down and go away. Cobras rise up and expand their hoods while rattlers coil and rattle their tails to discourage further interaction. They hope that you will back off, but they are prepared to strike if you don't. "He blinked" or "turned tail" are acknowledgements of people's reactions to such displays or threats.

Skillfully identifying a bluff requires an appreciation of the psychology underlying it. A bluff is an attempt to create a false impression intended to disguise a person's true belief. People who bluff generally overcompensate, as they attempt to manipulate how confident they appear. They are trying to create the opposite impression of how they truly feel, and this creates perceptible incongruence (Lieberman, 2000). The person, who bluffs by stiffening or pushing away from the negotiating table, often does so too quickly. He is like a stage actor trying to adjust to movie acting. He knows that he has to make sure that you get the message, but he overdoes it. He either does it too "loudly," or too abruptly. The disparity between his true feelings and the message he hopes to convey creates internal tension, which is evident in excessive muscle tension and irregular, shallow breathing.

The person who breathes naturally while becoming erect or positioning himself to strike is not bluffing. He is congruent. His true objective is either to leave or strike, therefore his statement is perceived as credible like when Jack Nicholson's says, "You can't handle the truth!" in the movie "A Few Good Men." There is no excessive muscle tension in Nicholson's delivery and even though he is shouting, he's in control of his feelings. He is neither whining nor pleading; he is merely making a loud, definitive assertion.

People will often betray their willingness to change their position on a topic by breaking their posture. This has been observed so frequently that it has been institutionalized in our language. We acknowledge this phenomenon when we say he "was moved" or "squirmed in his seat." Each expression describes an emotional shift or a predisposition to change positions in a negotiation. It is not just the movement that is important. The timing of the movement in relation to what has just transpired and the way the person breathes before or as they move is also important. These behaviors represent opportunities to gain concessions in the minds of many skilled negotiators. They appreciate the law of inertia that states that a body at rest tends to stay at rest and that a moving body tends to continue to move in that direction. Once someone has moved in your direction, you want to keep him or her moving. Sometimes any movement will do, particularly when the person won't give any indication of what they think. Talk in response to a question is a minimal form of movement – which is why salespeople will ask you what you think of something. Their reasoning is that as long as you are moving, they can guide you to move in a particular direction. "No talk, no opportunity."

People considering a new mental image (position) will often blink repeatedly as they survey new possibilities. Of course, not everyone blinking is processing pictures. It is important to consider the situation, what is happening at the time, and whether or not this is a new behavior. Blinking can sometimes be an effort to adjust to an unexpected circumstance. A few years ago, a senior manager tried to force me in my capacity as an internal management consultant with the company to support a position that greatly favored his prospects for promotion. He talked with the executive who oversaw my activities, and later my manager, in an effort to force my hand. To this day the senior manager does not know what happened at our subsequent encounter. When the large group in which he was a participant met for its next scheduled all-afternoon meeting, I started by reiterating my role and responsibilities to the group and nonverbally letting him know that I was standing my ground. Using a visual FAP, I let him know that he was the target of the message, but no one else was aware that I had singled him out. Shortly after my statement, he turned red and started to blink and wipe his face from brow to chin repeatedly. Within minutes he had dismissed himself and left. He did not return that day. His behavior was a little more dramatic than just blinking, but it accomplished the same thing. One interpretation of his behavior was that he had a clear image (with feelings) of what he expected and was visually and kinesthetically trying to adjust to what confronted him. Regardless of what his behavior meant, he never again tried to force me to do anything.

Much of this book is about the people's physiological responses to actions and activities that trigger emotional responses in interpersonal interactions. Among the many signs of emotional impact are: skin color, gesticulation, and posture. Skin color is a good indicator of changes in mood. The most obvious colors are, of course, red and white. People generally turn red when they are embarrassed or angry, even sad.

People generally turn white when they are very surprised, scared, hurt, or upset. As with any nonverbal behavior, it is important to both know the person's normal color (baseline) and whatever is occurring around them that may be stimulating the change. Incidentally, people of color respond with changes in their skin color, too. Only the darkest skin does not change color. The range of color change will be smaller than among people with light complexions, but it will occur. A brown-skinned person can actually turn a shade of purple, instead of red.

Some parts of the anatomy change color faster than other parts. I have noticed in negotiations that the scalps of people with crew cuts often indicate internal changes before their faces. One negotiator's scalp turned red long before his face did and he was unaware of it. He knew when his face was turning red, but not his scalp. His scalp's color was an important "tell." In fact, redness washed over him from his scalp down to his face.

In a negotiation over the disposition of nuclear waste, a federal agency chose to be represented by an inexperienced young, female engineer. This young woman had been out of college for less than five years and was now negotiating with men with 10 to15 more years of experience in nuclear operations, and who held positions several levels above her in their respective organizations. I served as a consultant to one of the stakeholders in the negotiations and observed an unfortunate pattern in this young woman. She had an obvious "tell." She signaled her distress in a negotiation by "splotching." Whenever she seemed to be surprised by a position (either the content of a proposal or the force of its presentation), didn't know an answer to a question, or didn't have the authority to commit her agency to an action, she would develop large, irregular red splotches on her neck. These splotches would increase in number and progress up and down from her neck, as she grew more uncomfortable. The fact that she had a very light complexion made this phenomenon very conspicuous.

People don't actually have to experience an event to reveal their feelings about it. When reliving or contemplating an event they will often exhibit the same changes in skin color and muscle tension that occurred or might occur in an actual situation. Skin color may become pale or flush as they experience the anxiety or excitement of a situation. This phenomenon can be used as a type of lie detector.

I Guess I Saw That Coming

The small talk phase of a negotiation can provide very useful baseline information. You have an opportunity to see how the person behaves in a relaxed state, and if you are observant and strategic, in an excited state. Observe their breathing and mannerisms in a relaxed state to determine their preferred modality. Asking questions about things that they like to do or reminding them of pleasant experiences will give you an idea of what they look like when they are excited. It is good to know what both of these states look like to understand their range of emotions during the negotiation. If possible, you would like to observe a full range of emotions including fear, pain, anger, and joy when calibrating their reactions. "What if" questions can broaden the range of their emotional display. Small talk has strategic importance because while emotional displays are fairly generic, the expression of emotions differs slightly. We really don't want to just be able to identify an emotion; we also want to be able to gauge its intensity.

Measuring Moves

The fact that the human body often reveals emotions before a person can express them verbally or attempt to actively suppress them can be used tactically in social interactions and negotiations. It is possible to suggest options in a situation and literally read which ones appeal to or repulse a listener-perceiver. This tactic can prevent unnecessary conflict and give the impression that the speaker-sender is in synchrony with her audience.

I used this tactic while negotiating with a military officer a few years ago. His hair was cut short enough that I could see his scalp. I found that I could prompt a response by announcing several possible actions or proposals, watch for his response to each one, and then make adjustments accordingly. If he started to turn red (his scalp turned red first) or the muscles in his jaw became visible, I would simply move to the next proposal. It is possible to slow or even stop a reaction, if you have timing.

Being proactive requires the ability to interpret subtle changes before they become big changes. Many people consistently exhibit subtle indicators of impending emotions or actions; and they are often unaware of these signals. Some of these signals include: quivering muscles in the chin as an indication of an inclination to cry; the tightening of muscles around the mouth or covering the mouth as an effort to suppress speech; and the pulsing of muscles around the temple as an indication of frustration. From a facilitator's perspective, many auditory people actually open their mouths before they start to talk – a behavior that can be a very useful cue for preventing the expression an untimely or inappropriate thought. An untimely or inappropriate comment can be not only be counterproductive, it can actually scuttle effort to achieve an agreement.

Artistry in the use of nonverbal behavior requires that you are not only able to identify emotions, but also that you can anticipate and avoid unfavorable emotional reactions. If you can see the signals that indicate the start of an emotion, you can sometimes change your course of action to prevent the person fully experiencing associated feelings. Good timing makes it possible to prevent or reduce the intensity of a reaction and thereby maintain control of the interaction.

Key #5

Skillful nonverbals let you be hard on a problem and soft on the people.

Don't Look at Him

Fisher and Ury (1981) advise negotiators to be "hard on the problem and not on the people." Conflicts often induce people to be abusive with each other and this is often counterproductive. It is possible to attack a problem without attacking people holding contrary views if you know how to manage your nonverbal behavior. It is also possible to make strong points and be tough without damaging relationships. One of the most important things to remember is that making a negative comment, irrespective of content, while looking at someone causes that person to take your comment personally. Where you look and when is important when you make your point. Harsh comments with eye contact damage personal relationships, so avoid making eye contact when you say something negative. The effective use of nonverbals makes it possible to have differences of opinion without enmity.

Tip #27: When setting boundaries or enforcing rules, it is best to talk as little as possible and use nonverbals to avoid the appearance of bullying.

Tip #28: Setting boundaries or managing misbehavior should be done with few words, and even less eye contact.

You can save yourself a lot of trouble by using diagrams and visual images to model complex problems. They are beneficial in three important ways. First, you can direct your unhappiness, disappointment, or aggression at the image and not a person. Second, they can allow you to make unflattering or blunt statements without directing them at another person. Third, pictures allow us to express complex thoughts efficiently. It is surprising how limited words are for expressing complex ideas. Furthermore, words take too much time when people are in disagreement. Most people are unwilling to give you the time to fully explain your thoughts or ideas when disagreement is intense. Even the most logical person will find himself trying to pick apart your argument as you present it, rather than trying to understand it. Less reasonable people will be preparing their rebuttal as you speak. A picture truly can truly be worth a thousand words.

Diagram of problems and solutions provide negotiators with at least two other advantages. First, an elaborate picture increases the likelihood of people having a collective understanding of a problem. And second, the act of constructing a graphic representation of a problem focuses attention on the problem and not the people.

Expressing resource limitations or resistance is best asserted without eye contact. These actions will be perceived as negative so avoiding eye contact is advisable. Instead of looking at the person, look at the document or an object that symbolically limits you (a prop). People are inclined to argue with you if you look at them while making your point. Not making eye contact reduces the likelihood of an argument about your point. If you are skillful enough to make the statement using a credible voice pattern you will also find that people will often accept that your assertion is not open for debate.

Process Softens Words

The only way to systematically be hard on a problem and yet soft on the people associated with it is to find a way to physically separate people from the problem. Trying to do this verbally often rings hollow as when U.S. government spokespeople immediately following 911 kept telling the American people that we were fighting Islamic terrorism, but that the government did not see Muslims or all Middle Easterners as evil. In spite of what the government was saying, many Americans saw all Middle Easterners as potential terrorists.

Of the three variables involved in human communication (content, process and emotion), we probably have the most control over process. The content is the substance of a conflict. It potentially can be reframed, but not at the onset of a dispute since it is often at the core of a negotiation or argument. Process refers to how we communicate – in other words, our verbal and nonverbal behavior. The third factor, emotion, is most elegantly managed by our nonverbal behavior.

The best way to avoid the presence of negative and counterproductive emotions is to manage our nonverbal behaviors. The way we direct our gaze, the way we use our voices, what we do with our bodies, and the way we breathe all affect the emotions in a negotiation or conflict. The simplest strategy, however, focuses on gaze behavior.

Separating people from the problem is best accomplished nonverbally. Making a representation of the problem, in the form of a model or a diagram, visually and kinesthetically separates people from the problem. The problem can now be positioned in front of us both. In fact, we can kinesthetically modify our relationship with each other by putting the representation of the problem in front of us so that we can view it shoulder-to-shoulder. Each of the parties no longer will see other parties as the problem, and they will unconsciously see themselves as partners dealing with it.

One of the reasons why creating a representation of the problem is so important has to do with another visual FAP. When person A expresses an opinion in opposition to person B while person B is looking at them, person A essentially becomes the problem in the mind of person B. The FAP seems to work by linking the speaker to the content. The utterance (position) becomes visually linked to the speaker.

Looking at the your "opponents" when describing a problem often encourages the formation of "protective circles." If there is more than one person present on a side, you can almost see the proverbial wagons circling. People in protective circles avoid personal responsibility for feelings, behaviors, and any resulting consequences (Paul and Paul, 1983). They stop being open to learning about themselves or others, which short-circuits collaborative negotiation since it depends on people learning about the needs or concerns of themselves and others. People trying to protect themselves are inclined to select from one of three responses: compliance, control, or indifference. Protective circles destroy trust and generally damage interpersonal relationships.

Compliance involves "rolling over and giving in." The person just conforms to what another person wants. He or she yields to another's demands to avoid disapproval or rejection. The nonverbal behaviors associated with compliance are an avoidance of eye contact, speech in a low almost inaudible voice, the use of few words, and a lack of enunciation. There is also a tendency for people being compliant to be hunched over and have long faces.

People getting other people to comply are often surprised by the difference between what people say they will do and what they actually do. Compliance in a negotiation rarely ensures compliance with the terms of a deal. People who feel that they were forced to comply often renege on deals; and those who do not renege have a tendency to practice "malicious compliance." In other words, they comply as long as they are being scrutinized. As soon as an observer turns his or her attention away from them, they go back to doing something different than expected or nothing at all.

If control is the chosen option, the person may counterattack immediately. However, more often than not, he or she will postpone the fight for another round. You can see the nonverbals of withdrawal such as physically moving away from others, talking to each other while other parties talk, or responding to proposals without pausing to give any consideration to its merits. A lack of a pause after the reception of a proposal can indicate that the proposal has been discounted or ignored. If someone who has chosen the control option thinks that you have more power than him or her, and he or she doesn't respond quickly to your assertion of force, you can expect to be ambushed.

People, who have chosen to be indifferent, generally mentally withdraw from the interaction. They may physically move away, become less punctual, and arrive unprepared.

In short, not managing nonverbal behavior in an interaction can have very serious consequences. It can stimulate negative emotions, intensify problems, and even derail social interactions.

Stepping Back

The secret to subliminally influencing others is artfully managing yourself. This is difficult to do because we have to manage our reactions and read the situation as it progresses. It is possible to prevent people from feeling the full force of an emotion by observing the cues that indicate the onset of the emotion. This requires paying attention to the effect of your actions (or those of others) on listener-perceivers.

People expressing their emotions are usually a positive sign in social interactions, but not always. Sometimes it is important to help someone save face by preventing them from publicly being overwhelmed by their emotions. These emotions can be anger or expressions of pain that lead to embarrassment. Cohen (1980) explains that there are two types of opponents in conflicts – idea opponents and visceral opponents. Idea opponents dislike our proposals or ideas and are willing to engage us to make changes, but visceral opponents are not. They hate their opposition. They cannot separate the person from the problem. Cohen points out that the quickest way to create a visceral opponent is to humiliate a person. Helping people save face can prevent social interactions from turning nasty.

If you can see the cues that indicate the start of an emotion, you can sometimes change what you are doing so that the person does not fully experience the emotion in public. The simplest action is to call for a break. If you still have rapport with the person, you can sometimes redirect their attention away from the stimulus that is generating the emotion. Highly skillful people can actually use their nonverbals to moderate the expression of the emotion by consciously slowing and deepening their breathing. None of these tactics can, however, be applied unless you monitor the feelings of others.

Key #6

Look for "pearls" in the gaps between what people say and what people do.

I'm Listening, Really I Am

Appropriate nonverbal behavior during active listening depends on whom we are interacting with (their state of mind and modality), how we are perceived in terms of role and status, and our objectives. Specific behaviors will elicit different responses from people according to the modality (visual, auditory or kinesthetic) they are operating from at the moment.

Your goal is also important in selecting the appropriate nonverbal behaviors for an interaction. If your focus is the substance of the message such as the wording and details, you may want to encourage them to use their digital (logical dispassionate) channel. If you sit erectly, avoid eye contact and use words like "assume," realize," and "logical," they will tend to act accordingly. If you are trying to get information about emotions, slower speech with a noticeably more relaxed body posture and limited eye contact will generally produce favorable results.

Matching their style can be used to encourage communication, although the converse can also produce results. That is to say that creating tension by behaving very differently than the listener can also stimulate talk under the right circumstances.

Reflective listening is valuable for ensuring that the meaning of what is said is understood. The expression "reflecting" refers to the process of paraphrasing what someone has said so that you can verify your understanding, and sometimes so that they can become more aware of their own emotions. Typically, people are taught to reflect until the listener says "yes." This is good advice even though you should be able to detect affirmation before they actually say yes. Their subtle head nodding (even when they don't want to) and breathing will confirm your paraphrasing before they ever speak. Having the person say "yes" is, however, valuable to prevent back sliding on a fact or issue as a tactic.

Nonverbal behaviors that interfere with the process of active listening or disturb people can be very counterproductive. For example, the wrong tone and posture while using a "door opener" (an action designed to encourage talk) can cause people to become reticent or defensive. Asking questions to encourage talk is always riskier than using nonverbal behavior. Head nodding, expressing puzzlement, and shrugging are all nonverbal behaviors that can encourage speech very effectively without words. Appropriate choices about how you use your eyes, voice, gestures and body must always be based on your objectives and your relationship with a listener.

People operating from different modalities sometimes resemble two people driving a car without talking to each other as one person operates the gas, brake and clutch pedals, while the other controls steering and shifting. Conversations lurch forward or are stalled and take unexpected turns. The stalling and lurching is sometimes related to problems with turn-taking, in other words, the exchange of roles from listener to speaker (Nofsinger, 1991). The greater the differences in communicative styles and the more stress in an interaction, the more likely we are to experience difficulties figuring out when to talk. Active listening requires paraphrasing and reflecting which means that you periodically have to talk. When to talk can be complicated when dealing with someone in an auditory or kinesthetic state. The auditory person can talk incessantly with very few pauses. This trait and their willingness to talk while you talk can make turn-taking frustrating. They have no problem talking as you talk until one of you concedes the floor.

Turn-taking can also be difficult when working with kinesthetic people because they take long pauses as they talk and sometimes draw words out to hold the floor. Since they don't tend to pause much, you will find yourself not wanting to interrupt but feeling the need as you seek to clarify their utterances. Turn taking problems notwithstanding, these interactions can be very tense because of the need for clarification since kinesthetics are not very discriminating about the words they use to describe emotions and situations. They also tend to focus on personalities and action more than logic making it difficult for non-kinesthetics to follow their arguments. Give the kinesthetic extra time to reflect before you talk. Touching them and then talking is one fairly effective way to get you the floor when talking with them.

Table 4 correlates behavioral preferences by modality and phase of active listening. It illustrates differences in preferences for eye contact, space (proximity) and other behaviors. Note that some of the generic recommendations about active listening often seen in basic books are not recommended for every modality (communication style). This is because different actions have very different impacts on people depending on their preferred modalities.

Proximity refers to our need for space. A visual person usually feels that his or her space has been invaded at the same distance that a kinesthetic feels comfortable. Always consider the distance between you and the other person when you or they gesture. Intruding on someone's space with a gesture can have very unpleasant consequences.

Many people find active listening to be artificial or uncomfortable because they are self-conscious about restating what others say to them. This fear is usually unfounded. Effective active listening provides five major dividends:

1. People deeply appreciate feeling heard.
2. Paraphrasing stops escalating anger and cools down crisis.
3. Paraphrasing stops miscommunication. False assumptions, errors, and misinterpretations are corrected on the spot.
4. Paraphrasing helps you remember what was said.
5. When you paraphrase you'll find it much harder to compare [your view to theirs, judge, rehearse your pitch, and derail their line of thought] (McKay et al, 1983:24).

Having disputants paraphrase each other is very effective for getting disputants to listen to each other. It makes it difficult for someone to emotionally remove himself from others or the topic. It also prevents him from being distracted and provides a good excuse for encouraging speakers to be succinct. You can gently urge the speaker to shorten his or her discourse to make paraphrasing easier. Auditories sometimes really need this kind of prodding. They often have difficulty being brief.

Table 3. Subtle Accessing Cues

Access Cue	Representational System			Indicated
	Visual	Auditory	Kinesthetic	Other specified
Breathing	Top of chest/rapid, jerky/shallow	Solar plexus smooth/even inhale and exhale	Abdomen/slow/deep	
Facial skin and muscle tone, skin color and texture	Raised brows/cheeks pulled upward/tight skin/less color in cheeks or spotty	Cheeks pulled toward ears	Jowls sagging/cheeks relaxed/color even in cheeks/even flush on face	
Moisture level on skin	Dry	Moister	Moistest	
Pupil Size	Smoothly varying	Little variation/slow variation	May show extreme dilation or constriction in rapid but infrequent size changes	
Pulse	Rapid/shallow	Very even rhythm/medium rate	Slow/deep/even/pulse may be highly visible	
Body postures, gestures	Upward head tilt/hand gestures upward shoulders up back and forth steps	Telephone postures with cocked head hand to ear/hand gestures at the abdominal level	Hand movements to lower body	(Gustatory) swallowing, lip and tongue movements weight on right leg-movement in right foot, hand (olfactory) flared nostrils
Voice	Higher pitch/varying rate and pitch	Even rhythm/even pitch/tone continuous	Lower pitch/slow/slowly varying pitch and rate	

Table 4. Situational Nonverbal Active Listening Skills

	Skills	Nonverbal Behaviors
Attending (V)	Eye Contact	K – Minimal V – Yes, important A – Neutral
	Open Position	K – Close proximity; relaxed, even though don't look at you much V – Lean forward; palms up A – "uh, huh"
	Head Nod	K – Neutral V – Neutral A – Yes, especially with eye contact
Reflecting	"You" Focus	Even, deep breathing Soft voice Smooth gestures
	Feelings	Voice and body consistent with emotion being expressed
Encouraging	Prompt	K – hand gestures; head nod without eye contact V – favorable facial gestures and eye contact A –lean forward with eye contact
	Door Opener	K – look down V – wrinkled brow; raised eyebrows A – head nod; "tell me more"

Ultimately, active listening moves a conversation or negotiation forward. It is a form of results-based listening that allows people to explore a situation and transition into problem solving and taking action. Transitions are always dangerous. You can mis-time a transition by approaching it too abruptly, or just stating the problem or goal incorrectly. They basically involve four parts:

1. State the problem (pause)
2. State the goal (pause)
3. Ask what's been thought of or done
4. Reflect

Two very important nonverbals affect transitions – voice patterns and pauses. Many people use either a friendly or authoritative voice pattern without consciously thinking about the strategic implications of such an action. Sometimes you will want to state the goal definitively, at other times you may want do so to invite discussion. What you do with your eyes, voice and hands will determine the strategic implications of your statement.

Your objective in active listening is to discover underlying issues, values, interests, and concerns. You can use a "door opener" to invite a person to start talking, then listen using attending and encouraging skills. Eventually, you will want to reflect both feelings and thoughts. Once people start to talk, avoid using questions to encourage them to continue. They often break the flow of their thoughts. If you must talk to re-initiate speech, it is important to realize that you need *not* finish your sentence. Fading toward the end of a sentence or pausing to invite a listener to finish a sentence often works well. You don't want to introduce any more of your words than necessary. Remember that you are looking for an accurate definition of the problem, and clear inferences about values and issues. You also want them to "own" what they say, so you do not want to put words in their mouths.

People who feel safe will allow you to explore their positions and interests. Once you have satisfactorily discovered someone's thoughts and feelings, you can restate problems, goals, and thoughts with reflection; and then look for permission to take action. An important strategic decision must be made at this point. Are you going to be directive as in asserting your needs and advancing unilateral proposals, or are you going to keep reflecting, ask questions and facilitating the creation of a joint solution.

Incongruity is a Pearl

Look for inconsistencies in what people say and do to gain real understanding. If someone says that she is receptive but is stiff and speaks in a detached manner, you know that something is wrong. She is being incongruous (her nonverbal behavior is not matching her verbal behavior). Her behavior suggests that there is something going on and that you need to explore her motivation. It is possible that part of her wants to agree and another part of her is apprehensive. Your job is to encourage the part that wants to agree and allay the apprehension of the other part.

Pay close attention to people's presentations of background information, responses to questions, and responses to proposals. People reveal their true interests in their physiological or bodily reactions. If something is important to me, I may reflect it in a change of posture (literally and figuratively), in a change in respiration rate, or a change in speech rate. These are all changes that are fairly apparent. Perceived threat in the form of interference with a goal, or an assault on the ego can often trigger "raw" reflex reactions. The clearest example of this sort of reaction occurs when people "snap" at other people.

Sometimes you have to help people discover their needs. People are quick to identify their positions, but not as reflective about their true interests or deep needs. Incongruous behavior can give you clues about those needs. For example I have seen people assert a position, but then repeatedly ask for things that indicate that another value is more important to them. Here the incongruity has to do with emphasis as indicated by repetition. The hidden assumption is that which I am most concerned about generally gets most of my attention.

Many times the voice tells you where to look for information. The person may say something more loudly or softly than everything else that precedes or follows it. This behavior is particularly significant if the behavior is inconsistent with a stated objective. Someone trying to make a strong point by using a weak voice is sending some kind of message. The meaning may not, however, be obvious without follow-up questions.

Your intuition will often alert you to inconsistencies. A couple of years ago, I mediated a meeting where one of the parties was overly assertive from my perspective. He would not only make his point, but also hammer his "partners" with it. This appeared to be his modus operandi. After our first meeting, he confided that he was intentionally overbearing to further his goal of not having to interact with the group in the future. He was being strategic. He wanted the others to deal with his subordinate and accomplished this by behaving in a way that was inconsistent with his immediate goal, but advanced his strategic goal.

Pay attention to the intensity that people use when speaking about an issue to discover their values. Remember that the more deeply held the value that they are asserting, the more emotional intensity they will display. Emotional intensity is usually reflected in someone's volume and rate of speech, as well as, the size of gestures. An associated general rule is that the more emotional intensity a person displays, the less negotiable the position being asserted.

Some people's gestures seem to naturally be incongruent. George Bush senior's gestures sometimes were the opposite of what he said. This happened frequently enough to become part of comedian Dana Carvey's parody of him. With people other than the former president Bush, you should be concerned about the real importance of an issue when a person says that it is small, but his gestures indicate that it is large.

Many times incongruence is revealed through a disproportionate response to a stimulus. Disproportional reactions of concern are typically very large reactions to relatively small stimuli. The size of the response can be expressed in the amount of words used to respond, the volume or rate of the reply, or the immediacy of the reaction. The following is an example from a recent radio call-in program on fetal toxicity from exposure to environmental chemicals. During the program, the author of a book on the topic stated that breast milk is the healthiest food for babies. Although she explained that breast milk could concentrate environmental contaminants, she commented that it was unfortunate that many women in the United States choose not to breast-feed their infants. She spoke about this topic for less than five minutes of a 40 minute interview before a woman caller in a strained voice (indicative of shallow breathing) explained that some mothers don't have time to breast feed and that she thought that the author's comments were made by people who want to make mothers feel guilty for going to work. Several nonverbal cues indicated that the author had struck a "nerve," or more accurately a *value*. The caller's emotional intensity was evident in her strained voice. She was having difficulty containing her emotions. Apparently, the caller felt victimized by the author's comments. She personalized the author's comments, and then accused the author of trying to create the feelings that she was experiencing. The main point, however, is that she focused on a 30 second casual comment and delivered a rebuke that was considerably longer than the comment. Additionally, the emotional intensity of her rebuke was very disproportionate to the comment.

Tip # 29: People's physical intensity often indicates their level of interest in a particular issue.

Pearls in the Gaps

Sophisticated communicators, mediators and negotiators pay attention to both what is said, and how and when it is said. If you just listen to what people say, you will often miss the real message. It is difficult, in fact artificial, to separate the verbal from the nonverbal dimensions of talk. Talk is composed of both, and some of the most important insights come from noting when the verbal and nonverbal dimensions of a message are in conflict. The range of things that are included in the nonverbal dimension is also much broader than what is covered by body language. Repetition of ideas, for example, can be considered to be a nonverbal cue.

Nonverbal behaviors provide collaborative negotiators and facilitative mediators with important information related to the prioritization of values and goals. Collaborative negotiations require that parties deconstruct their positions and find common interests or needs. These needs are closely tied to their values. Nonverbals provide these negotiators with cues about priorities. Negotiators can see the signs of pain and pleasure as long as they pay attention to the nonverbal behaviors of others. This can often be detected in the intensity and recurrence of themes in talk. People will rarely reveal their priorities consciously for fear that others will take advantage of them, but they do reveal them unconsciously through their voices, gestures, and physiology.

Incongruence, which is when verbal and nonverbal messages do not match, is one of the most valuable indicators of the internal dynamics of individuals. Expressions like "yeah, right" or "thanks, for sharing" are examples of incongruent communication. People who tend to prefer to avoid conflict or be accommodating will often respond to a direct question about what is bothering them with comments like, "nothing" or "I'm okay," but with nonverbal cues that are not congruent with the words. Incongruence is a sign that you must dig deeper.

There are two different schools of thought regarding incongruence. The first school believes that we should only trust nonverbal messages when they are in conflict with verbal messages. This argument makes sense because people cannot control their nonverbal behavior as well as they can control what they say; so if you have to choose one over the other, it makes sense to trust the more reliable source. Another school of thought believes that *both* the verbal and the nonverbal message are expressions of truth. From this perspective, incongruence is a reflection of internal conflict (Kostere and Malatesta, 1989). Regardless of which school you agree with, incongruence should promote interest in people's motivation.

Incongruence also can be seen among complexes of nonverbal behaviors. Someone can be extending his hand to you after making a verbal agreement, give you a firm handshake, and yet avoid eye contact. These apparently contradictory nonverbals can be a sign of mixed feelings or a signal that more needs to be said. Then again the person may be distracted by something happening behind you. More data is required to draw a reliable conclusion.

Table 5. Verbal and Nonverbal Congruency

	Verbal	Non-verbal
Disputant:	It sounds like a good deal.	Head shaking back and forth, voice tone weak
Disputant:	I'm angry at Tom.	Voice tone quiet and soft, breathing slow and even
Disputant:	No problem, I don't mind picking it up.	Flat, tight voice with shallow breathing

The verbal and nonverbal portions of the communications above indicate mixed feelings. Conflicting messages offered at the same time are referred to as *simultaneous incongruency*. When examining these conflicting messages, considering each subpart or paramessage of the message is valuable. Disregarding the verbal in favor of the nonverbal may lead you to overlook a repeating theme.

In other cases, the conflicting message is communicated by the phrase following the other in sequence. This form of conflicting message often occurs within the same sentence and is referred to as *sequential incongruency*.

Example: I like her, but she drives me nuts.

In this case, there are two paramessages in conflict.

Paramessage:
1. I like her.
2. She drives me nuts.

It is difficult to determine the actual meaning of the second paramessage without noting other nonverbal cues in the speaker. The speaker could be incongruent in terms of saying that he likes her, but then implying even more intense feelings for her. Or, he could be saying that he likes her but she also upsets him. Only other nonverbal cues will allow someone to comfortably interpret the message. The speaker's accompanying tone, facial expression, or hand gestures would probably clarify such a message.

Example: I trust you, but I want it in writing.

Paramessage:
1. I trust you.
2. I want it in writing because I don't fully trust you.

Sequential incongruity provides the possibility of paramessages that are themselves either congruent or incongruent (Kostere and Malatesta, 1989).

Table 6. Paramessages in Talk

Verbal	Nonverbal
I have worked well with him for six years.	Smile on face, even breathing rate, firm steady voice tone/head nodding up and down
He's easy-going and helpful.	Voice strained, lips pulled tight, brow furrowed, head nodding up and down

In this example, the first paramessage offered is simultaneously congruent, but the second message offers conflicting data between the verbal and nonverbal communication channels. It is not uncommon for people to try to protect someone's image by saying a half-truth and hoping that you are unable to discern truth from falsehood.

Values are Visceral

People reveal their values verbally and nonverbally. All values are standards with emotional charge. In other words, values are felt viscerally. We acquire values slowly and insidiously through socialization, mainly through informal instruction and trial and error. Some important values can be articulated explicitly with little difficulty, but many other values are unknown to us unless someone violates them. Values about deference and demeanor often fall into this class. For example, you may not know that you have rules about how secretarial staff members are supposed to address you until a secretary addresses you by your first name while referring to his boss as Mr. Thompson. All of a sudden, you can become indignant, fueled by the energy of violated values.

It is not unusual for people to be unaware of, or want to deny, some of their values. Some of our values when made explicit are not very appealing to us. Take for example an interaction I had while working as a trial consultant a few years ago. We were talking about cultures and their impacts on decision making and I told her of a simple, but powerful model that I had developed. I suggested that she would operate according to the values of "elites" in her professional life. The trial consultant denied that she saw herself as an "elite" person – a term for describing a member of a hierarchical culture. I was explaining how the term was part of a cultural model I used for categorizing the values of prospective jurors and told her that we were both members of this cultural group because we held advanced degrees. In fact, anyone with a license, certification, or a union card is an "elite" when they operate according to the rights, privileges, and responsibilities that their credential or affiliation with an institution gives them. She insisted that she was not an elite – Americans tend to not like the term – so I decided to demonstrate my point. I asked her to imagine that she was being introduced in a room full of physicians and that the person making the introductions says, "This is Dr. Thomas, Dr. Rodriguez, and Ms. Hiller referring to her (not here real name). Just as I said this, her body stiffened, the muscles in her face tightened, and she turned red. I smiled and innocently asked, "What's wrong?" She could hardly speak and sharply exclaimed, "I hate that!" What she hated was the tendency for some physicians to not acknowledge the fact that she too was a doctor, albeit not a medical doctor. She perceived this to be unfair and she could not conceal her body's visceral response to the insult.

Values defining the concept of fairness are deep values, and consequently inspire dramatic and immediate physiological responses. She may not have normally viewed herself as an elite, but her body registered that in that context she saw herself as a member of an elite group.

Deep values are always discernible in social interactions. When violated they can be seen in changes in behavior. Some people freeze, some people lose track of what they are saying or doing, some people lose color in their faces while others may suddenly gain color. The point is that there will be a noticeable change.

It is important to note that not all values are equal. Some values are deeper than others. The deeper the value, the less likely people will deviate from them. Deep values are often associated with issues of fairness and justice. They are standards about how things should be done. Fortunately, many deep values are not mutually exclusive. In fact, Hans Bleiker (1986) has suggested that most important conflicts can be resolved by framing the dispute using a deeper set of values. For example, people may disagree about a specific outcome, but they are often willing to agree that another party has a right to have their interests protected in a decision making process. In fact, some of our deepest values have to do with beliefs about our rights and responsibilities as well as those of others. Most Americans have common beliefs about the freedoms and rights of citizenship. They also tend to have a common appreciation of the obligations of citizenship, although they must sometimes be reminded of them.

Watch, listen and learn. People reveal what is important to them in a variety of ways ranging from subtle to conspicuous behaviors. With practice the subtle will become conspicuous.

Key #7

Use space; don't let it (ab)use you.

Location, Location, Location

Location, location, location is not only the most important factor in real estate, it is critical in negotiations and complex social interactions. The idea of a "home court" advantage is commonplace in sports competition and negotiations and clearly reflects a belief in the connection between performance and location. Some locations make you feel good or perform better. Sometimes that performance is not inspired by good feelings as much desperation – someone with his back to the wall fights much harder than someone with an escape route. If locations can make you feel good, they can also make you bad when they become "contaminated" by bad memories. The idea of contamination is based on a fixed action pattern related to locations. The human mind associates an intense feeling with the places where it occurred. An extraordinary or repetitive experience can also be associated with a place. Once feelings have been linked with a particular place, that person will automatically re-experience those feelings upon entering that space again.

It is best to avoid space that makes you feel bad. Along those lines, having a business meeting in the same room where your last sales pitch flopped is not advisable. Seek places that inspire good performance, or at least, that can be considered neutral ground. Some locations are contaminated by virtue of the mental associations people have of the work that takes place there. Hospitals, dentists' office, and mortuaries easily come to mind. Professionals working in these settings have to consider the effects of the settings themselves on people. For example, physicians should be aware of the fact that clinics and hospitals typically intimidate non-medical people. Very bright people will often find themselves unable to answer simple questions about their reason for scheduling an appointment or facts about the course of an illness, in part, because of the stress of being in the medical facility. The association of the space with pain or feeling alien certainly doesn't help people's thought processes.

Good physicians try to overcome the stress of the location by adjusting their bedside manner. One way to do this is by using space and touch. Sometimes a physician can help a patient to think by moving in close to them without eye contact and talking in a relaxed manner. Other times, it may require standing side-by-side with them to talk about a situation. Thinking about space and how you move in it can decrease the negative impact of a location and increase people's capacity to think, respond, and relax.

Just to Be Close to You

Proximity affects interpersonal relationships in a variety of ways. It can nonverbally communicate the emotional strength of a relationship, it can reinvigorate a relationship, and it can even create the circumstances for new relationships. For example, oftentimes, being in a new location creates opportunities to forge new relationships or modify old ones.

Experienced mediators sometimes have parties meet in isolated locations and assist them establish and strengthen new relationships. This is particularly important when trying to help entrenched parties realize their interdependence. The lack of interruptions and distractions and the lack of an audience to inspire grandstanding makes it possible for people to actually listen to each other and work to understand each other's concerns.

Space can also give you an idea of the nature of the relationships between people. People often hint at their emotional or positional closeness in negotiations through their use of space. They may sit closer to the people they like, they may shoulder-to-shoulder with allies, or they may sit across from their opposition. A few years ago, I watched a senior manager abruptly and literally push himself away from a meeting table as he realized that a "field person" was about to give his team a briefing. He sat away from the table and leaning back in his chair through the whole briefing. After the man left, he expressed his displeasure at having had to listen to a briefing from a "knuckledragger."

Don't Step in It

A location doesn't always have to be a room or large space. It can be a spot or small area in a room such as a podium or a dais. Any spot can be contaminated by bad feelings. A few years ago, I was asked to give a plenary speech at a conference for the Society for Professionals in Dispute Resolution (now the Association for Conflict Resolution) in Seattle. A former colleague and mentor, Bill Lincoln, was to give the keynote speech and I was to immediately follow him with a talk about culture. I had not seen Bill in years and was happy to hear that he was going to speak to the organization. Unfortunately, Bill hadn't had much of a chance to prepare a speech; he had just returned on a "red eye" flight from the East coast when he realized he had this commitment. I was told that he had spent the day before trying to talk Senator Jesse Helms out of taking punitive action against Cuba for shooting down an American aircraft that had violated its air space. Anyway, Bill was in a foul mood by the time he got to the podium. He spent 40 minutes telling us how we should not be patting ourselves on the back for being mediators when none of us had made any real efforts to prevent injustices in the world. He was particularly upset about the United States' apparent lack of interest in atrocities being committed in Bosnia at the time. He described some of them in detail. Surprisingly, at the end of what felt like a pummeling, he invited us to a mediation workshop he was conducting later in the month. Given the effect of his speech on the audience, I doubt many people went to the workshop, which is unfortunate because he is an exceptional trainer. What Bill had managed to do was contaminate himself, the podium, and his presentation location with negative feelings, which was now my problem because I was expected to talk immediately after him. People seemed perplexed when I insisted on speaking from the other side of the room and not using the podium. Had I not done this, I too would have been contaminated by his speech. People would have associated me, and my topic, with bad feelings irrespective of what I said.

Size and Placement Matters

Semi-fixed features in a space are environmental structures that are not permanently fixed such as seating or furniture arrangements. They can be very important nonverbals. Aside from the issues of status related to positions in a room, seating arrangements are important because they affect the prospects for eye contact, audibility, and the effect of movement on others. For instance, sitting to the side of person can prevent eye contact, thereby limiting the effect that you can have on him or her, or limiting their ability to read you. Seating positions are important because there are times when you may want to be able to look directly at a person or make eye contact to emphasize a point or gauge the sincerity of what was said, among other things.

Tables and chairs can sometimes used for protection. Spaulding Gray, the late great monologist, was asked in a radio interview if he ever felt uncomfortable revealing so much of himself to an audience. He replied, "No, that's why I have a table." He saw the table, oftentimes the only thing on stage with him, as a protective barrier.

Pay attention to space. It has many potential uses depending on the knowledge and skill of a speaker-sender. It can be used to increase the memory of an idea by creating a location for the memory, transform speakers, and to change subjects. Many people are unaware that television news anchors assist viewers to recognize transitions to new news items by visibly shifting positions (locations) in their seats or turning to face a different camera.

The dynamic aspects of space are the result of the interplay between people communicating with each other. It is important to pay attention to the amount of space between people in relation to how they move and gesture. The large gestures of kinesthetics can shock people, even other kinesthetics, when they are executed in confined spaces. Abrupt movements in small spaces tend to increase tension and anxiety.

Of course, the size of a room can greatly affect interpersonal interactions. I once made the mistake of mediating a dispute between three people in a windowless, 5 x 5 foot room. We were packed so tightly around a three-foot round table that the parties could easily smack each other – and at times, I thought they might. The room seemed to intensify their emotions, and the fact that there was so little space between the table and the wall made all of us feel trapped.

It is often not the actual size of the room, as much as the population density of a room that affects interpersonal dynamics. A densely crowded room will almost always have an effect on kinesthetic people. If the people in the room are close friends of the kinesthetic person, the crowding just makes encounters that much more fun and intense. However, a room full of unfamiliar people can create great stress in kinesthetics.

The collective energy of people in a room can be dissipated in a sparsely populated space or a room not built to a human scale. When a room dwarfs people, they don't feel like they are in control of their surroundings. It is for this reason that architects tend to design restaurants and residential spaces using an intimate scale (where sizes are slightly, but perceptibly, smaller than one expects them to be) to convey an impression of cozy shelter. The intimate scale gives an observer "a pleasant sense of ease; he feels that his environment is readily manageable and that he can relax. Part of his reaction, also is a gratifying increase in his awareness of his own importance as an individual. He feels larger and more powerful in an environment whose elements he can cope with so effortlessly" (Raskin, 1966:45,46).

The size of a room also affects people's ability to perceive nonverbal behaviors. If the room is too large, listener-perceivers may not register a hand gesture or the relative position of a speaker to an object. The listener-perceiver can also be expected to have difficulty hearing subtle changes in volume, tone, or diction. This could diminish the effect of an auditory FAP. And of course, a cramped room can force movement to be reduced in range and size, which can drastically affect the impact of a presentation.

Shape Matters Too

Not only does the size of a room matter, so does its shape. A few years ago, I gave a talk in a very strange room at a major hotel. The room was configured so that it was about 18 feet deep but 40 feet wide. I had given the same talk to part of the organization in a standard sized room and was now delivering it to members of a group that had missed the earlier presentation. The second presentation was very different than the first. The fact that the front row of the audience was within five feet of me, meant that I had to adjust my volume so as not to overwhelm them. Unfortunately, doing this made it difficult for people at the far ends of the room to hear. The people in the first row were so close to me that it also forced me to reduce the size of my gestures so as not to literally put my hands into their faces, and I also couldn't move around as much as I liked. The effects of lowering my volume and reducing the size of my gestures were evident to people in the audience. The few people that had been at the earlier presentation told me that I seemed "subdued" and less engaged in this one. Others commented the presentation was "okay" but "felt kind of flat." Nothing in the presentation had changed except for my ability to move and project my voice; but in reality these were huge changes.

My ability to nonverbally influence the group was severely diminished by the dimensions of the room. Expansive gestures can energize a group, but they can also cause stress if they encroach on people's personal space. Modulating the tone and volume of a presentation helps members of an audience maintain attention as it allows a presenter to emphasize some points, punctuate others, and draw the audience in. The changes in my nonverbal behavior reduced the dynamism of the talk and dampened the impact of some of the points being expressed.

Another important problem associated with the bizarre dimensions of the room had to do with the difficulties it imposed on my ability to read the room. There was no vantage point from which I could see the whole room. My field of vision was not broad enough to allow me to see the people on the wings when I was in the front and middle of the room. Looking from one side or the other meant losing the opportunity to observe the nonverbal behaviors of large numbers of people.

If I couldn't see them, then they couldn't see me. In other words, the impact of gestures and other actions that are perceived visually were compromised. Worse yet, the inability of some people to see me created the potential for having differential effects on the audience as some listener-perceivers received very different messages during the interaction. Even auditory signals were compromised by efforts to avoid appearing to shout at some people to ensure that distant members of the audience could hear.

Light Me Up

Lighting affects a negotiation and social interaction. Natural light seems to energize social interactions. People feel more energetic in a room with natural light. When there is a low level of energy in a room, there is a tendency toward intransigence amongst its occupants.

Natural light also enhances people's sensory acuity and ability to maintain attention; two critical factors in reading nonverbal behavior. The constantly changing nature of daylight automatically and naturally responds to the body's need for a change of stimuli or mood. The human body is not adapted to steady stimuli. It needs change. If the environment doesn't change, it responds by changing itself. For example, the pupil of the eye will become dilated or constricted even under conditions of constant and uniform brightness, thus giving the impression of varying brightness. When stimuli is monotonous, as under conditions of artificial light, "the body's *ability* to respond to stimuli will gradually deteriorate until subtle changes cannot be perceived at all. People require changing stimuli to remain sensitive and alert" (Evans, 1981:21).

Read the Room, Read the Person

People reveal a great deal about themselves in the placement of objects in a home, office, or conference room. The placement of objects is a tangible manifestation of thinking styles. For example, visual people reflect their interests in order, color coordination, and neatness by the way they arrange and maintain their offices. Their offices are often neat; pictures are aligned and objects are organized and arranged by size or color. Rarely will you encounter a visual person with a cluttered office. If you do, you should be concerned because it usually suggests that they are overwhelmed or struggling.

Furnishings in a visual person's office are often chosen for their look. Visuals like clean lines. They also like high contrast colors such as blacks, whites, dark blues, and reds. It is not unusual for them to have attractive, but not very comfortable furniture. For them, space is meant to project an image more than to be comfortable. They are much more inclined to put their certifications, awards, and degrees on their walls than kinesthetics.

Kinesthetics, on the other hand, often have cluttered spaces. They often have piles of materials all around their offices. Their offices are a form of organized chaos, but there is a sense of order at work; it's just based on locations. Kinesthetics generally know what is in each pile and like archeologists know exactly which stratum contains a particular file.

A kinesthetic's office is designed to be comfortable. Furniture has to feel right and the things around them are positioned to make them feel good. Knickknacks, awards, and memorabilia all have the capacity to alter their mood when manipulated, so they'd rather have them on their desks than on their walls.

If kinesthetics have pictures, they are not there for aesthetics as much as for feelings. Pictures of kids, vacation spots, or fishing trips are typically on display, as opposed to pieces of fine art. It is not unusual for them to proudly display the artwork of their small children.

The offices of auditory people vary greatly. One of the most salient clues about an auditory person's space is the presence of a radio or stereo. Auditory people often like background music because they tend to work more efficiently while listening to it. An auditory person's office space is difficult to characterize because it seems to feature a combination of visual and kinesthetic traits.

Too Close for Comfort

People who are predominantly visual, auditory and kinesthetic have very different preferences for the use of space. In fact, these people actually experience space so differently that they define spaciousness, crowdedness, privacy, and appropriate and inappropriate distances very differently.

People have expectations about how space should be used for casual conversation, intimate talk, and formal presentations. These distance zones are determined by a combination of cultural and idiosyncratic expectations. Violating a person's spatial requirements can create discomfort and elevated levels of stress. As stress increases there is a notable decline in a person's ability to listen attentively. There is also a tendency for the person to react without thinking and to take actions that appear to provide immediate relief of some discomfort but often without consideration of longterm consequences. The violation of proxemic expectations, or norms, results in consistently disruptive effects on the communication between two or more people" (Leathers, 1992:111).

For example, standing too close to a visual person actually induces stress. Many North Americans experience this kind of stress when they go abroad. People in the Middle East and parts of Europe, when comfortable with you, will tend to want to be much closer to you than the average American as they talk.

Different ethnicities have different culturally-defined spatial needs. Visuals, like Scandinavians, prefer to be far apart from each other while conversing. They want to see the whole of the person. Kinesthetics, like Greeks, want to be close enough to touch each other. Clashing preferences can cause stress. Being too far away for a kinesthetic or too close for an auditory will cause stress in them.

Failure to take proper account of spatial factors can lead people to have unnecessarily challenging interactions. Increasing the distance between yourself and another individual as you interact can damage the level of satisfaction associated with newly formed relationships. In other words, it can create a negative impression and damage interpersonal trust. Conversely, "individuals who use mutually preferred interaction distances facilitate the development of satisfying interpersonal relationships" (Leathers, 1992:112).

Crowding can also have a negative impact on your ability to establish and maintain satisfying relationships with other people. It can intensify negative energy and actually increase the likelihood of conflict among people.

Back to the Woodshed

There is an expression that, "locations have memories." This refers to the fact that people tend to link feelings – good and bad – with places. It is important not to try to solve a problem in the same space it was created. People may not consciously realize that there is a problem, but their bodies will. Sometimes you don't have the luxury of seeing someone contaminate the space, but you should be aware of the possibility that you are operating in contaminated space.

The effect of previously contaminated space became very apparent in a conflict I intervened in about five years ago. A man and a woman who worked together for a couple of years were having difficulties partially based on differences in communicative style, but also exacerbated by a significant difference in age. Although these two people had different duties and worked for different organizations, they had to work together on some cooperative programs. Early in their relationship, the man had taken the woman, who was the age of his oldest daughter, "under his wing" and helped her to understand the programs and their constituencies.

Whenever the man perceived that she had made a political mistake or wanted to give her advice, he would ask her to meet him in a conference room on the floor above their offices. At these meetings they would discuss what was happening, why, and what they could do to change things. He would try not to be judgmental or directive, but according to her, he could not help conveying that he wasn't happy by the sharpness of his questioning or his frowns. After a while, he found that she started avoiding the meetings or would say very little to him at the meetings. He became concerned and then requested meetings – always in the same room – to discuss why she was avoiding him. When I asked her about the meetings in the conference room, she admitted that she hated to go to there. She said that every time he requested a meeting there, she felt that she was "being taken to the woodshed." The space was contaminated and it triggered very bad feelings in her.

Unfortunately, I didn't learn about her feelings about the room until after we had had a mediation session with she and her colleague in the room she hated. From the moment she entered the room, it was clear that the interaction was going to be very difficult. She literally could not breathe from the moment she sat down. She turned bright red, swallowed frequently, and her voice was barely audible as she choked out responses to my questions. Her nonverbals were so powerful that I felt compelled to have them change positions in the room. I later found out that she had initially sat where she always sat during his sessions, and so had he. I encouraged them to move by using a whiteboard at the other end of the room and suggesting that they reposition themselves in order to see it. This change in seating allowed her to take her eyes off of her colleague, enabling her to breathe and subsequently think. Spots in rooms are often contaminated, and slight changes in the positions of participants are sometimes all that is necessary to separate them from these contaminated areas.

It is wise not to negotiate in a contaminated space. Bad feelings from previous interactions will often contaminate subsequent interactions and cause people to start discussions with "an axe to grind."

Reminder: Don't locate the problem in the same space as the solution; separate them.

Time Out, So You Don't Space Out

Herb Cohen admonished people to never negotiate with themselves in front of others. This was very sound advice. Negotiating with yourself in front of others makes you vulnerable to dirty tricks and impulse decisions. You can avoid this problem by using space effectively. Before you negotiate, decide how you want to use the negotiation space. Designate a separate place for reflection and relaxation. When you are confused or sense too much tension, call for a break and retire to your space.

Skilled competitive negotiators want you to negotiate with yourself in front of them. They try to change your position by forcing you to adopt their reference points or they introduce extraneous fact into your deliberations. One such ploy is to get you to consider the cost of an item in terms of dollars per month, instead of total cost. This forces you to have to make calculations in front of them. When someone throws you a curve, take a break and go to your designated space to think. It is to your benefit to place references and other materials in this designated space.

Mediators can save themselves implementation problems by preventing situations where people are forced to negotiate with themselves in front of others. If you see the nonverbals of confusion, consider giving negotiators the opportunity to take a break or caucus. Buyer's remorse is often associated with people not feeling confident about their choices because part of them feels that they acted without enough consideration. Getting some distance from the engagement can diminish the likelihood of buyer's remorse.

Tip #30: Designate a space for reflection and dealing with confusion. People negotiating with themselves are vulnerable.

Tip #31: A new location helps "decontaminate" an idea or proposal.

Closing Thoughts

The keys to influence are fairly complex, and are best learned through trial and error. Just as you use one key at a time to unlock doors, it is reasonable to think about, and practice one key at a time. The main idea is to see its application, and experiment. Test the effect of using different approaches to accomplish the same objective and see what happens. The keys give you a way to plan an interaction, be systematic about your actions, and have a framework for forensic analysis. Progress is measured in terms of how quickly you recognize that something is going well, or badly, and what you do to improve or maintain the situation. When you first practice, you'll find yourself saying, "I should have done this or that." Have confidence that in time you will be saying, "that was a good move, I wonder what made me do that."

References

Adams, Damon. Doctors urged to mind bedside manners. AMNews, March 21, 2005.

Ambady N., LaPlanta D., Nguyen T., Rosenthal R., Chaumenton N., Levinson W. Surgeon's Tone of Voice: A Clue to Malpractice History. Surgery 2002:132(1):5-9.

Asimov, Isaac. 1966. *Understanding Physics*. New York: Barnes and Noble.

Ballentine, R. 1976. *The Science of Breath*. Glenview, IL: Himalayan International Institute.

Birdwhistell, R. L. 1970. Kinesics and Context. Philadelphia: University of Pennsylvania Press.

Bleiker, Hans and Annemarie Bleiker. 1986. Citizen Participation Handbook for Public Officials and Other Professionals Serving the Public. Laramie, WY: Institute for Participatory Management and Planning.

Blakeslee, Thomas R. 1980. The Right Brain. Garden City, NY: Anchor Press.

Bodenhamer Bob G. and L. Michael Hall. 1997. Figuring Out People. Bancyfelin, Carmarthen, Wales: The Anglo American Book Company.

Bradshaw, John. 1985. *The Family*. Deerfield Beach, FL: Health Communications, Inc.

Bretto, Charlotte. 1988. A Framework for Excellence. Capitola, CA: CPD.

Brooks, Michael. 1989. *Instant Rapport*. New York: Warner Books.

Carnavale, P.J. and R. Pegnetter. (1985). The selection of mediation tactics in public sector disputes: A contingency analysis. *Journal of Social Issues*, *41*, 65-81.

Cialdini, Robert B. 1993. *Influence: The Psychology of Persuasion*. New York: Quill William Morrow.

Clatterbuck, G. (1979) Attributional confidence and uncertainty in initial interactions. *Human Communication Research*, 5, 147-157.

Cohen, Herb. 1980. *You Can Negotiate Anything*. New York: Bantam Books.

Connor, Tim. 1981. *The Soft Sell*. Ann Arbor, MI: Training Associates Int'l.

Couturier, Laurent, Stephen Hacker, and Marsha Willard. (2000). *The Trust Imperative Workbook*. Blacksburg, VA: Insight Press.

Crum, Thomas F. 1987. *The Magic of Conflict*. New York: Touchstone.

Csikszentmihalyi, Mihaly. 1990. Flow. New York: HarperCollins Publishers.

Damasio, Antonio R. 1999. *The Feelings of What Happens*. San Diego: Harcourt, Inc.

Dana, Daniel. 1989. *Managing Differences*. Wolcott, CT: MTI Publications.

Ehrlich, Paul R. 2000. Human Natures. Washington, D.C.: Island Press.

Ekman, Paul. 1992. *Telling Lies*. New York: W.W. Norton.

Evans, Benjamin H. 1981. *Daylight in Architecture*. McGraw-Hill, Inc.

Everly, Jr., George S. 1989. *A Clinical Guide to the Treatment of the Human Stress Response.* New York: Plenum Press.

Fisher, Roger and William Ury. 1981. *Getting to Yes.* New York: Penguin Books.

Freed, Jeffrey and Laurie Parsons. 1997. Right-Brained Children in a Left-Brained World. New York: Simon and Schuster.

Goleman, Daniel. 1995. *Emotional Intelligence.* New York: Bantam Books.

Goffman, Erving. 1967. *Interaction Ritual.* Garden City, NY: Doubleday & Company.

Grandin, Temple and Catherine Johnson. 2005. Animals in Translation. New York: Scribner.

Grinder, Michael. 1991. *Righting the Educational Conveyor Belt.* Second Edition. Metamorphous Press: Portland, OR.

Grinder, Michael. 1999. New Trends in Learning Styles. Michael Grinder & Associates.

Hall, Edward T. 1983. *The Dance of Life.* New York: Doubleday.

Hampden-Turner, Charles. 1981. *Maps of the Mind.* New York: Macmillan Publishing, Co.

Herrmann, Ned. 1995. The Creative Brain. Lake Lure, NC: The Ned Herrmann Group.

Howard, Pierce J. 1994. *The Owner's Manual for the Brain.* Austin, TX: Leornian Press.

Hunsaker, Phillip and Anthony J. Alessandra. 1980. *The Art of Managing People.* New York: Simon and Schuster, Inc.

Hymes, A. 1980. Diaphramatic breath control and post surgical care. Research Bulletin of the Himalayan International Institute, *1*, 9-10 cited in Everly, Jr., George S. 1989. *A Clinical Guide to the Treatment of the Human Stress Response.* New York: Plenum Press.

Jamieson, Kathleen Hall. 1992. *Dirty Politics.* New York: Oxford University Press.

Karim, A. and R. Pegnetter. (1983). Mediator strategies and qualities and mediation effectiveness. *Industrial Relations, 22,* 105-114.

Keesing, Felix. M. 1959. *Cultural Anthropology.* New York: Rinehart & Company, Inc.

Kelly, Kevin. 1994. *Out of Control.* Reading, MA: Addison-Wesley Publishing Company.

Kostere, Kim and Linda Malatesta. 1989. *Get the Results You Want.* Portland, OR: Metamorphous Press.

Kouzes, James M. and Barry Z. Posner. 1995. *The Leadership Challenge.* San Francisco: Jossey-Bass.

Kreger Silverman. 2002. Upside-Down Brilliance. Denver, CO: DeLeon Publishing, Inc.

Kressel, K. (1972). *Labor mediation: An exploratory survey.* Albany, NY: Association of Labor Mediation Agencies.

Leathers, Dale. G. 1992. *Successful Nonverbal Communication.* New York: Macmillan Publishing Company.

Lee, Linda. 1975. *The Tao of Jeet Kune Do.* Burbank, CA: Ohara Publications.

Lee, Scout. 1990. *The Excellence Principle.* Portland, OR: Metamorphous Press.

Lieberman, David J. 2000. *Get Anyone To Do Anything.* NY: St. Martin's Griffin.

Levin, Edward. 1980. *Negotiating Tactics.* New York: Fawcett Columbine.

Lewis, David. 1989. *The Secret Language of Success.* New York: Carroll & Graf Publishers.

Mangin, René-Marc. 1989. *A Multidisciplinary Systems-based Analysis of the Timber/Fish/Wildlife Environmental Policy Negotiations.* Doctoral dissertation, Washington State University.

Maruyama, Koretoshi. 1984. *Aikido with Ki.* Tokyo: Ki No Kenyukai H.Q.

Meister Vitale, Barbara. 1982. *Unicorns Are real.* Rolling Estates, CA: Jalamar Press.

McKay, Matthew, Martha Davis and Patrick Fanning. 1983. *How to Communicate.* New York: MJF Books.

Merman, Stephen K. and john E. McLaughlin. 1983. *Out-Interviewing the Interviewer.* Englewood Cliffs, NJ: Prentice-Hall, Inc.

Moyers, Bill. 1989. The Public Mind: Image and Reality in America, Illusions of News. A Production of Alvin H. Perlmutter, Inc. and Public Affairs Television, Inc.

Nofsinger, Robert E. 1991. *Everyday Conversation.* Newbury Park, CA: Sage Publications.

O'Connor, Joseph and Ian McDermott. 1997. *The Art of Systems Thinking.* San Francisco: Thorsons.

Paul, Jordan and Margaret Paul. 1983. *Do I Have to Give Up Me to Be Loved By You?* Minneapolis: CompCare Publications.

Pearce, Joseph Chilton. 1977. *Magical Child.* New York: Plume.

Rayl, A.J.S., Humor: A Mind-body Connection. The Scientist, 14 (19):1, Oct. 2, 2000.

Pratap, V., Berrettini, W., and Smith, C. (1978). Arterial blood gases in pranayama practice. Perceptual and Motor Skills, *46*, 171-174 cited in Everly, Jr., George S. 1989. *A Clinical Guide to the Treatment of the Human Stress Response.* New York: Plenum Press.

Raskin, Eugene. 1966. Architecturally Speaking. New York: Bloch Publishing Company.

Rinn, W. (1984). The neuropsychology of facial expression: A review of the neurological and psychological mechanisms for producing facial expressions. Psychological Bulletin, 95 (1), 52-77.

Roach, Christopher J. 1991. The Effectiveness of Selected Mediator Strategies on the Resolution of National Forest Plan Appeals. Master's thesis. Central Washington University.

Robbins, Anthony. 1990. *The Science and Art of Human Influence.* San Diego: Robbins Research International, Inc.

Rush, Sarah. 2000. *The Language of Trees.* Rush's Arts: Ojai, CA.

Satir, Virginia. 1972. *Peoplemaking.* Palo Alto, CA: Science and Behavior Books.

Sapolsky, Robert M. 1994. *Why Zebras Don't Get Ulcers.* New York: W.H. Freeman and Company.

Shadow, Michael. 1988. Notes from a Pacific Institute training session.

Sibley, S. S. and S.E. Merry. (1986). Mediator settlement strategies. *Law and Policy, 8,* 7-32.

Slater, Hal. 1993. *First Call Closing.* La Jolla, CA: BBP Publications.

Springer, Sally P. and Georg Deutsch. 1993. Left Brain, Right Brain. New York: W.H. Freeman and Company.

Stein, Joel. (2003). Just Say Om. Time, August 4, 2003.

The Learning Channel. Deception. Television program aired Nov. 2002.

Thompson, J.G. 1988. Cited in *The Owner's Manual for the Brain* by Pierce J. Howard 1994.

Torres, Jose. 1989. *Fire & Fear.* New York: Warner Books, Inc.

Viscott, David. 1976. *The Language of Feelings.* New York: Pocket Books.

Warshaw, Tessa A. 1980. *Winning By Negotiation.* New York: McGraw-Hill Book Company.

White, Ron. 1999. How Computers Work. Indianapolis, IN: Que Corporation.

Williams, Frederick. 1984. *The New Communications.* Wadsworth Publishing: Belmont, CA.

Yamada, Yoshimitsu. 1969. *Aikido Complete.* Secaucus, New Jersey: The Citadel Press.